THE MAKING OF HERO

Praise for *The Making of Hero*

'Amongst entrepreneur families, the Munjal Brothers deserve a special place in India's history. With little or no support from the government or otherwise, Brijmohan, whom I knew well and respected, managed to build successful businesses through diligence, dogged pursuit and an incredible ability to develop relationships and partnerships across the manufacturing value chain. The fact that they achieved success with complete integrity is what makes *The Making of Hero* special. Sunil has spun together a wonderfully detailed and personal story.'

Ratan N. Tata, ***Chairman Emeritus, Tata Sons***

'I was very fond of Brijmohan Lallji and have often publicly referred to him as my Guru. Brijmohan Lallji had amazing qualities of head and heart and was really a unique individual. Sunil has captured his ability to lead by example and to fill others around him with his spirit and enthusiasm.'

Rahul Bajaj, ***Chairman, Bajaj Auto***

'The narrative is set across a vast landscape, and since I have interacted with many in the Munjal family, I was able to relate to a lot of it. The book's down-to-earth focus and underlying messages on managing businesses, families and relationships are interesting and timeless. My expectations from this book were quite high, and I am not disappointed.'

Sunil Bharti Mittal, ***Founder and Chairman, Bharti Enterprises***

'At a time when Indian manufacturing barely had any legs to stand upon, Hero Cycles and subsequently Hero Honda showed how these legs could be built with a strong mind and a stronger heart. Self-belief, to my mind, was the single biggest contribution made to Indian industry by Mr Brijmohan Munjal and his brothers as they built Hero. Sunil has woven together a remarkable story of struggle and triumph based on the bedrock of humility.'

Anand Mahindra, ***Chairman and Managing Director, Mahindra Group***

'It was fascinating to read about how the Munjal brothers shared a similar philosophy and culture of high efficiency and productivity while running a business in the most humane manner. In *The Making of Hero*, Sunil offers

THE MAKING OF HERO

FOUR BROTHERS, TWO WHEELS AND A REVOLUTION THAT SHAPED INDIA

SUNIL KANT MUNJAL

HARPER BUSINESS
An Imprint of HarperCollins *Publishers*

First published in hardback by Harper Business
An imprint of HarperCollins *Publishers* 2020

HarperCollins Publishers India, Cyber City, Building 10-A, Gurugram,
Haryana-122002, India
www.harpercollins.co.in

This edition published in paperback in India by Harper Business 2021

2 4 6 8 10 9 7 5 3 1

P-ISBN: 978-93-5422-737-0
E-ISBN: 978-93-5302-678-3

Cover design: HarperCollins *Publishers* India
Front cover photo and author photo: Courtsey of the author

Typeset in 12/16 Adobe Garamond Pro at
Manipal Technologies Limited, Manipal

Printed and bound at
MicroPrints India, New Delhi

MIX
Paper
FSC FSC® C218906

This product is made of FSC®-certified and other controlled material.

HarperCollins Publishers, Macken House, 39/40 Mayor Street
Upper, Dublin 1, D01 C9W8, Ireland

To my parents

My mother, my guide
My father, my hero

To my anchors and the future

My wife Mukta, daughter Shefali
&
My twin grandchildren, Alena & Ishaan

Contents

FOUR BROTHERS - FOUR GENERATIONS

***Dayanand Munjal**
***Vedwati**

Achla	Sonia Rajeev Sareen	Sanchit Viren
**Devender Hingle*	Vinay Hingle Rachna	Yajush Shaurya
Vijay	Naveen Vandana	Shivom Saina
Rekha	Gaurav Samita	Shrihaan
Ashish	Neeti Davinder Singh (Sunny)	Dabeet Simar
Shobhna	Aman Ruchi	Aarav Aaira
Ashok	Roshni Nitin Passi	Leissha Saessha
Neelam	Chandni Sumit Arora	Savanna Amaara

***Satyanand Munjal**
***Pushpavati**

Yogesh	Neeraj Charu	Avi Yajan
**Harsh*	Nidhi Rajesh Kapoor	Madhav Sadhak
Suresh	Sameer Anu	Sumantra Aradhya
Rama	Gautam Swati	Akshat Daivik
**Sushma*	Vikas Chopra Bhavika	Prisha Krishay
Jitender Chopra	Rishi Chopra Sheetal	Aashna Atharav
Sudhir	Anuj Rinkle	Shaurya Lavanya
Anju	Aarti Ajay Chowdhary	Akansha Jasmine
Neelam	Reena Vishal Dhir	Yajur Kyna
Arun Thapar	Uday Thapar Divya	Aarav Ashmita
Umesh	Amol Deepti	Kanish Ameera
Urmil	Ankur Divya	Divyank
Mahesh	Aashima	
Renuka	Aayush Amiya	

***Brijmohan Lall Munjal**
***Santosh**

**Raman* Renu	Rahul Pooja	Sarthak Siyona
	Radhika Saurabh Uppal	Kavishaa Krishav
	Abhimanyu Saloni	Aadiv Ahaan
Geeta	Gaytri	
	Arjun Tania	Abeer Reeba
Suman Renuka	Ujjwal Sonaal	Jaiveer Suveer
	Akshay Swati	Anandni Meher
	Vidur	
Pawan Aniesha	Vasudha Pankaj Dinodia	Shiv Syna
	Supria	
	Annuvrat	
Sunil Mukta	Shefali	Alena Ishaan

***Om Prakash Munjal**
***Sudershan**

Neeru Suresh Khanna	Ruchika Vikram Bakshi	Shivika
	Varun Khanna Natasha	Yashvir Anya
Neeta Rajendra Seth	Shradha Amit Manaktala	Amyra
	Sidhant Seth	
Punam Sanjeev Soni	Bharat Soni Kanika	Prisha Maisha
	Kunal Soni Aditi	Vivaan Viraj
	Vibhav Soni Disha	
Pankaj Munjal Charu	Aditya Aishwarya	
	Abhishek Ruhani	
Mridu (Priyanka) Pravin Malhotra	Nipun	
	Manek	

Boxes with no family name are all Munjals
**Deceased*

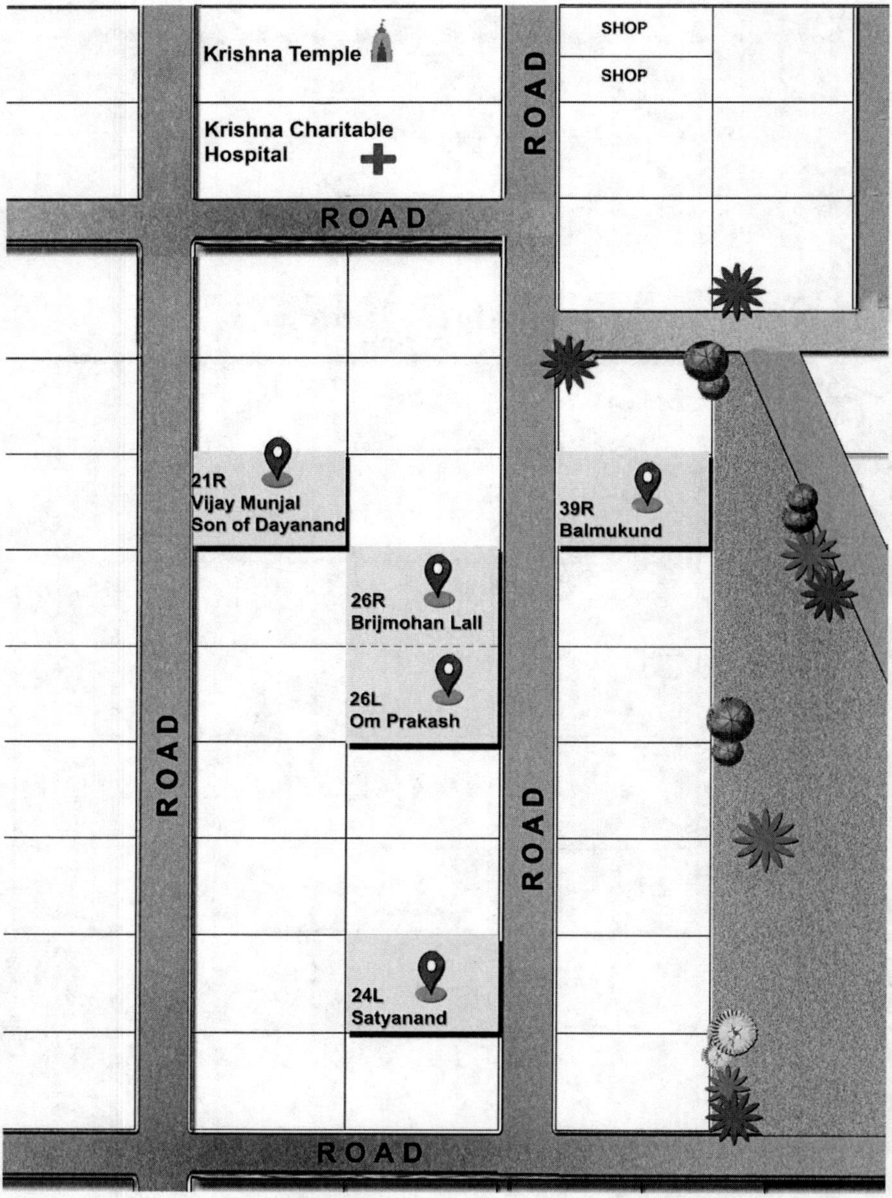

An artist's impression of the lane in Model Town, Ludhiana where the Munjal brothers lived in close proximity.

A Tryst with History

Tracing the Hero Roots

Some time ago, I got a call from a former diplomat friend of mine, who said that his *Maasi* (maternal aunt) read an article about my father and the family originating from Kamalia (now in Pakistan), and that she was keen to connect with someone who was conversant with India before Partition and reminisce about the old days as she was from Kamalia as well. The call rekindled a flood of memories from our younger days of hundreds of conversations about incidents we heard around the dining table and on other occasions about our family's history. Kamalia in district Lyallpur, which later became district Faisalabad and then district Toba Tek Singh (now in Pakistan), is where our family's recent history, as we know it, began – so this story has its roots in pre-partition India.

This book was in the making for many years. Over the previous decades, several people met my father and many of us, and expressed their eagerness and desire to capture his life story, and that of the Hero Group. On each occasion, in his inimitable manner, my father refused, saying it would go against the grain of the family culture to talk about oneself. In any case, he insisted that the Hero story was not his alone but belonged to the larger family, of which he was only one constituent. It's a different matter, though, that many believed he was the major catalyst for Hero's growth and development, and the pivot for the forward-looking business practices, sustaining the culture and crafting a space for Hero in public life.

Many people approached me to convince my father; but he held out, till after he turned ninety. The selected would-be authors were busy penning another book and sought some time to start work. Unfortunately, my father's health and time ran out before the project could be commissioned.

The requests to write a book about him continued to pour in even after he left us. I then realised that if a book needed to be written, it had to be done from the ringside, from close quarters. Also, rather than get a pedigreed author or a renowned business historian, I felt it needed the close involvement of those who knew my father and the family for most of their lives.

Even as I gathered my thoughts and decided to take the plunge myself, another interesting development took place. It was serendipity that S.K. Rai (managing director, Hero Cycles—Rai Sahab, as he is popularly called), who joined in the early 1980s and is considered an important part of the family, articulated his plans to write a similar, but broad-based book that encapsulated all the Munjal Brothers. I saw merit in this logic because it aligned with my father's own persona and his symbiotic ties with my uncles. While Hero was being built, critical decisions were taken by the brothers together; and responsibility for success and failure was shared. In my father's eyes, the brothers were a team; they were part of the same crew and each brought something unique to the navigation wheel. Moreover, their unique strengths and skills were in synchrony and in complete harmony. I then decided that this would be a story about my father, his brothers and the entire family.

My younger uncle Om Prakash had an astonishing capacity for numbers and relentless follow-up. He was also able to build amazing relationships with a larger community of dealers. My elder uncle Satyanand was the moral compass of the entire family and the organisation. He brought great empathy to whatever he did, whether it was dealing with workers or suppliers or building and operating schools and institutions for the *Arya Samaj* reformist movement. Dayanandji, who was elder to Satyanandji, passed away in 1968 just as Hero Cycles was moving to its new location where it resides even now. He had early on established a culture of extreme integrity and responsiveness. On his passing away, his son Vijay was considered amongst the senior members, along with the three elders.

Mr Rai graciously shared the material that he had gathered for me to use in the book that is in your hands now, and he could well be designated as a co-author for parts of this book.

This book is written in the form of multiple stories that flow into each other, and attempts to capture the evolution of the family, and how the Hero Group first learnt to walk, and then grow wings. It also puts these stories in the context of what was happening both politically and economically during different phases in India, and on the margin, also covers certain world events of that era.

Naturally, since my father and uncles were born in undivided India, and as the first Hero enterprise itself came up more than six decades ago, we ran into a few potholes while validating and authenticating the many facts and events of that era.

Visualising a picture of India just before and after Independence, which was when the Munjal brothers were setting out in life and in business, was quite a task. How could I fully picture a nation with a population of 390 million and fewer than 100,000 telephones, where one rupee was the same value as a US dollar, where gold was ₹88.62 per 10 grams, where you could buy 1 acre of land for ₹17,000 in South Delhi and rent a two-bedroom apartment in Bombay (Now Mumbai) for ₹40-50 per month!

The lack of records was another key hurdle. There is hardly any documentation of what happened during the early decades. Till the nineteen sixties, my father and uncles were too busy trying to provide for the family and build a sustainable business; they had neither the time nor enthusiasm to pen down their thoughts and rarely gave media interviews. The verification became more difficult as most people born in undivided India have passed away, while many others were still green behind their ears at the time. I have relied upon many of the incidents and stories that my mother, father, uncles and other family elders narrated; yet there were still a few gaps that needed filling. Also, in a family saga such as this, there are often multiple versions of the same incident. For instance, there was a debate whether it was my cousin Jatender's grandfather or my paternal grandfather's cousin Satish Dhingra who was my father's partner in one of my family's first businesses in Delhi.

I began what proved to be a long line of conversations with other family members, friends and elders. A typical example was Amrit Nagpal, a close and trusted friend of uncle Om Prakash and my father. He had worked closely with my uncle in the social service organisation of Lions Club and with my father in Dayanand Medical College and is now involved with me. Amrit considered my father a humanitarian and shared a similar vision for medical education and patient care.

My elder brother Suman helped me on several occasions to relive the past. My mother – who sadly passed away in early April 2021 as this edition was being planned – pulled out fascinating incidents from the recesses of her memory about her years with my father and his brothers, some dating back to her marriage just after India's Partition, and even earlier.

My cousin Yogesh (Satyanandji's eldest son), who was the only one in the second (our) generation to study in Kamalia, recounted crucial anecdotes from the early years which he knew and also those he had heard from his father Satyanandji and others; he and Suresh (Yogesh's younger brother) also helped me build the narrative through the 1960s. Likewise, Yogesh's youngest brother Sudhir plugged the gaps during the moped production days of the 1970s and we exchanged notes on how this laid the foundation for Hero Honda's later success. Dayanandji's son Vijay gave me some insights on his father, which were especially useful, since he had passed away in 1968. He also found a diary owned by uncle Dayanand that helped us validate some of the earlier dates and milestones.

Even after these conversations, there was a need to verify some of the incidents or fill some gaps, so I spoke to some senior present and retired executives of the companies, as well as government officials and others in the community.

Amit Chaturvedi who unfortunately passed away a few months after the book was published, came aboard as project manager just before the joint venture with Honda was set up. He had travelled to Japan with my father and my late eldest brother Ramanji to finalise the joint venture and headed the marketing function in the early years. My elder brother Pawan also joined the negotiations later. Amit's narration of incidents in the first decade of operations were quite useful, and funny on occasion. When my father went for his first meeting with Honda, the Japanese served him green tea and my father insisted on his masala tea, sending the Honda officials into a tizzy! Of course, during the second visit, masala chai was served in advance!

Rakesh Vasisht, who joined in 2000 as executive assistant to my father, and later to Pawan, detailed my father's hands-on role and his personalised style of management in the company, such that everyone felt he was the family elder in their lives.

I also had a chat with Jatender Mehta, my maternal cousin and one of Ramanji's closest friends whose firm was amongst the first ancillary units to shift from Ludhiana to Dharuhera to be part of the Hero Honda supply chain. Jatender reconfirmed some of the finer details of what was happening with the ancillaries in the 1980s and 1990s. He helped me to reaffirm how our larger family and the ancillary companies embarked on one of India's major quality-driven indigenisation programmes in the automotive industry.

As we approached the celebration of my father's ninetieth birthday, I asked many of his acquaintances, family members, friends, colleagues, suppliers etc, to write a letter to him about their relationship with him. I asked them to mail the letter to me instead of sending it directly to him because we wanted to compile these letters into a single publication and surprise him with this *Book of Letters* as a meaningful gift. The response was quite overwhelming; and our original plan of sending a copy of the book to each letter writer had to be changed as too many of the letters were emotional, touching and extremely personal. It felt ethereal to see just how many people felt a special connection with him; many spoke of the favours he had done for them without looking for recognition or seeking anything in exchange. The *Book of Letters* in many ways defined his personality and character so we decided collectively as a family to publish only one copy to present to him. For many months subsequently, it became a ritual that he would read one letter during the day in his office, and one at one in the evening along with my mother.

Besides my brothers Suman and Pawan, others who have shared interesting nuggets for this book include my sister Geeta, cousins Neeta and Mridu, and many other cousins, nephews and nieces. The two who provided inputs and helped with some corrections while suffering my poring over notes for many hours during family travels and holidays were my wife Mukta and daughter Shefali.

Senior journalist Bhavdeep Kang helped put the story through a chronological filter, and broadcast journalist, Shaili Chopra also contributed. Finally, from my team, Ashwani Sharma did numerous follow ups and connected with various stakeholders while Jaideep Lahiri anchored the project and helped me build the narrative. I am also very thankful to Sachin Sharma and Krishan Chopra of HarperCollins Publishers who have been very supportive and patient as we iterated and developed multiple versions of the narrative each with significant changes and, I believe, progressively better. Besides the story, as I know it myself, I have relied on multiple sources of research data, including case studies on Hero companies and our family's style of business which have been done by Institut Européen d'Administration des Affaires (INSEAD, France), London Business School, BBC, to name a few.

The reason this book has the word 'revolution' in its title is that when we look back, many of the things my father and uncles did were way ahead of time. They created a revolution not just in terms of the products, but also the culture they introduced, the productivity levels they set, the way they managed inventories and current assets, the quality levels they insisted upon, the manufacturing and marketing innovations they encouraged, the sustainable practices they swore by, the governance standards they set, the relationships they entered into, the integrity they believed in – every aspect of all the best practices that are now considered contemporary in the world of business and management were fully in place and operational in all parts of the Hero Group for over half a century.

The other revolutionary aspect of the Hero story was the best practices it triggered and the resulting knock-on effect on first the engineering, then the manufacturing scene and finally on the overall economy of India. The best practices were first shared with many of the suppliers and dealers; and later emulated in parts or whole by many from within and outside the industry.

As the policy space got created in India, due to economic and administrative reforms in the early 1990s for a widening of excellence in manufacturing, the private sector began taking on a larger responsibility in the country's industrial development, and Hero and its universe played a key role in accelerating the process. While in their lifetime they never bragged and were loath to talk about themselves yet there is little doubt that the transformation triggered by the Munjal brothers was the precursor for Made in India or Make in India, with excellence, and with pride—along with a few other leading institutions of the country.

This book seeks to preserve the legacy of our founders and to tell the story of how an organization shaped aspirations, pioneered large scale manufacturing and strengthened the nation's connections with the world. I only wish I could have written more. Despite the many incidents and stories narrated in this book, there are hundreds, and possibly thousands, that have not been included either to maintain a single flow to the book, or to maintain confidentiality in some cases, and most of all, to limit the book to a certain size on the advice and insistence of the publishers.

Some would call this a management book, others would say it is a family business saga still others would describe it as the story of a pioneering family enterprise whose six-decade old practices are contemporary, timeless and relevant even today. This could also be described as a history book, or an account of Corporate India's evolution or even India's story. I would say it is simply a family story with a heart and a personal labour of love. I hope you cherish reading this book as much as I enjoyed putting it together.

Whether you are a student of history or economics, or a manager or a teacher, or just somebody interested in a good yarn – I hope that you will take away and treasure something from the pages that follow.

Sunil Kant Munjal, October 2021

Foreword

by Dr Manmohan Singh

Brijmohan Lall Munjal epitomized the entrepreneurial spirit of Independent India. Displaced by Partition, he and his brothers arrived in Punjab with empty hands and a heart full of determination. Through sheer force of will, they made good, and in the process, transformed the landscape of India.

The Munjal brothers literally set the wheels of progress turning by popularizing affordable private transport. Hero's bicycles and two-wheelers combined quality with economy to offer unprecedented mobility to an India aspiring for growth.

The story of the Munjal brothers is not just a testimony to the indomitable human spirit, but also to the uniquely Indian community-oriented approach to business. Brijmohan Munjal and his brothers belonged to a generation of entrepreneurs that believed in the credo of learning by doing. The brothers ran their enterprise like a giant family and prioritized people and profits together in a symbiotic relationship. In their view, the greater good went hand in hand with profitability. In many ways, they were pioneers of many of the business practices that are common today. Just-in-time (JIT) inventory, triple bottom line (TBL), arms-length-related party transactions, independence of board members etc., are just some of the modern interpretations of practices that they had already established.

Their journey began in an inhospitable business environment. In the late 1940s, exhausted by two centuries of deindustrialization, India was overwhelmingly dependent on agriculture and was characterized by extreme poverty, sluggish capital formation, a pathetically low level of productivity and a snail's pace growth across private enterprises.

In the 1950s and 1960s, Pandit Jawaharlal Nehru's emphasis on state control in finance, a strong public sector, import substitution and industrialization set India on a growth trajectory, but the environment for business was not really conducive.

The Munjal brothers set up shop, undeterred by shortage of raw material, unavailability of technical expertise and limited access to institutional finance. They proved that India could compete with the best in the world, with courage, innovation and a 'can do' approach. The economy inched forward and, with it, Hero as an enterprise. Over time, policies changed, and the Munjals adapted as they went along.

An entrepreneur to the core, Brijmohan Munjal thought ahead, anticipated demand, created markets and set the agenda for the automotive industry. He was also one of the first to appreciate the value of working with and learning from foreign companies. At the same time, he understood the importance of skilling the available domestic talent so that they could imbibe and replicate the technology while still maintaining international standards of quality, and in many cases improving over what was seen overseas, all at very moderate prices.

Brijmohan Munjal's vision was global, even though his feet were rooted firmly in the Indian business ethos. He not only established one of the first and certainly the most successful business partnerships with a multinational firm, he also set Hero on the path to becoming the world's largest manufacturer of bicycles, and later, of two-wheelers and several component businesses.

As an industry leader, he took a holistic view of the economy and had no reservation in lobbying for changes in government policy that were good for the entire industry and for India. A staunch supporter of economic liberalization, which he felt heralded a marked change in the government's attitude to business, he was always positive and excited about India's prospects.

Brijmohan Munjal never attended business school. Indeed, he was not even a college graduate. Yet he was, and will always be, a role model for entrepreneurs and practitioners of management for generations to come.

The management skills of Brijmohan and his brothers – whom I had the pleasure of meeting on a few occasions – were derived from common sense, observation, experience, a hunger to learn and a regard for others. The brothers combined a range of hard and soft skills, but regarded empathy as the most valuable leadership tool. Brijmohan once told me that he and his brothers had learnt this at their mother's feet.

The Munjal brothers were trailblazers. Institutes of eminence across the world have studied the Hero Group's corporate philosophy, seeking to understand the extraordinary efficiencies, productivity and industrial relations that it engendered.

The Munjal brothers were pioneers in other ways as well. Long before corporate social responsibility (CSR) became a buzzword, they appreciated the importance of giving back to the community and took the lead in education and public health initiatives. Gradually, Hero's presence in the social sector expanded to include vocational training, skill development, sanitation, gender advocacy and many other fields. Similarly, sustainability concerns were addressed long before they became mandatory.

Besides being a visionary, Brijmohan Munjal is remembered as a disarmingly warm human being, completely free of arrogance or malice. This was a quality that I saw in him during all our interactions, and I have seen it endear him to people from all walks of life, be it bureaucrats, politicians, fellow entrepreneurs, or even family members.

He was a family man at the very core. Even when I was invited by him on formal occasions while I was prime minister, a number of family members were always present. In fact, his definition of family went beyond relatives to include all those who inhabited his vast circle of friends and business associates. His geniality and large-heartedness invested him with the aura of an elder statesman, and he was revered by business rivals and associates alike. He dispensed advice and held hands in times of grief and celebrated successes as if they were his own. The same courtesy and informality applied to Hero's consumers and dealers. However large the corporation became, it was never an impersonal or faceless behemoth. Its benign and smiling face was that of Brijmohan Lall Munjal.

In fact, I am delighted that the family has set up the BML Munjal University in his name to propagate his beliefs, ethos and best practices. That Sunil has accepted to be the chancellor, ensures that these are fully enshrined in the day-to-day practices of the university. I had plenty of occasions to interact with Sunil during his term as president of the Confederation of Indian Industry (CII), and also in the ten years when he was a member of the Prime Minister's Council for Trade and Industry, and I know that he is quite determined about preserving and sustaining the legacy of his father and uncles.

I am glad Sunil has found the time, effort and passion to authentically relive his family's story against the backdrop of India's economic and social history. He has packed in many fascinating facts and anecdotes and packaged them in a simple, interesting and easy-to-read format. As for me, I can personally empathize with the narrative, since I lived through the era.

Reading this book will provide many invaluable lessons based on real-life experiences of building a family, a business and playing an active role in nation-building.

Foreword

*by Arun Jaitley**

The Partition of India, although generally recalled in terms of its enduring evils, gave rise to a new breed of heroes. The refugee-entrepreneur who, through hard work and pioneering zeal, scripted his up-by-the bootstraps success story and in the process, created industry, infrastructure and jobs critical to a fledgling nation. Brijmohan Lall Munjal was one such hero.

Make in India is part of today's popular lexicon, but the Munjal brothers were its pioneers. Hero Cycles was set up in 1956; in thirty years, it became a world leader; Hero Honda became a world leader in seventeen years from its inception in 1985. In the manufacturing sector, I doubt if there are any better examples of leadership in multiple companies by a family enterprise anywhere else in the world.

---

* A special thank you to Shri Arun Jaitley, a statesman and former Finance Minister of India, who penned this message in July of 2019 after going through the book's manuscript. Unfortunately, we lost him before the book's release, and this foreword has been published with permission from his family. – Sunil Kant Munjal

Brijmohanji was distinguished as much by his sound business judgement, prescient vision and global outlook, as his old-school values. He and his brothers enjoyed an extraordinary connect and empathy with the consumer, worker, dealer and supplier, whom they viewed as members of their 'parivaar'. This connect, more than anything else, helped put a Hero cycle in millions of Indian homes in the decades before economic liberalization, and ensured continued success after reforms in 1991.

The Munjal brothers survived and thrived across multiple eras of change and churn. They lived in an era where people's ability to survive defined the course of their lives. They built a manufacturing enterprise at a time when money, machines, parts and know-how simply wasn't available. They never once veered away from values they believed in, such as honesty, integrity, respect for the individual and fair play, even in a business environment with stifling regulations and restrictions, where circumvention of rules was de-rigueur.

Adversity brought out the best in the Munjals. In the first three decades after Independence, a period where imports were prohibitive and technology transfer was virtually impossible, they innovated and developed an indigenous manufacturing system, and a foolproof way to manage current assets and liquidity (Just In Time or JIT in today's parlance).

In the 1980s and 1990s, when the entry of multinationals and cheap imports – mostly from the Far East and South East Asia created conditions for Indian companies to either sink or swim – the Munjals raised the bar and became dramatically more efficient. They invested in value engineering, built a high-class supply chain, levered their strong ties with dealers, and applied their knowledge of the Indian customer to grow much faster than the rest of the industry.

This book is a fascinating account of how a small, homegrown outfit grew from a small shed in Ludhiana into a global organization that impacted millions of lives. It celebrates the triumph of Indian values, spirit and enterprise. At almost seventy years of age, Brijmohanji brought to bear decades of experience, leadership skills and an intimate knowledge of markets to make Hero Honda an important part of India's growth story. By the turn of the millennium, he was at the helm of the world's largest two-wheeler company.

I have known Brijmohanji for many decades. I found that he was not just ahead of his time in gathering ideas, technologies and governance practices, but he also had an affectionate and warm way of getting the best out of people.

I saw him win friends and build relationships with people across ages, ethnicities and social strata, and I am told he did this through every phase in his life. He was able to carry many others with him as he walked up the stairs to success. Remarkably too, this success sat lightly on his shoulders.

All through, he remained the quintessential Punjabi: large-hearted, family centric and gregarious. He combined a hard head for business with a soft-hearted approach towards his fellow men and women.

His generosity of spirit and commitment to the larger cause of India's economic and social growth won him considerable goodwill, not just in the government and society, but even among direct competitors in the cycle and two-wheeler business.

The contribution of Brijmohan Munjal and his brothers went beyond the confines of business and industry. They set an example for the corporate world in philanthropy and inculcated the same values in their heirs, who have carried this legacy forward. Today, Hero is known for its sponsorship of a variety of sports, education, vocational skills, healthcare and efforts towards promotion and conservation of Indian arts and culture.

The exceptionally successful policies and processes that the Munjal brothers put in place have become the stuff of research papers and case studies worldwide, though no study can adequately capture the essence of the men who were the life and soul of the entire operation. To understand their essential humanity and breadth of vision, one must look behind the glaze of charted growth and profitability; and this is why this book becomes so relevant for students of business, management, history and general readers alike. Like me, I am sure they will thoroughly enjoy experiencing this remarkable journey that begins in undivided India, and travels through eight fascinating decades.

Even as Sunil has painstakingly traced the evolution of his family and business enterprise, he has set the story against the backdrop of what was happening in India and the world at the time – which provides a genuine perspective.

Today, as we prepare to enter the second decade of the new millennium, Sunil has ensured that the life lessons from the House of Munjals are not lost, and are now part of a collective legacy of wisdom that can power the dream of a new India, and many Indians and non-Indians in the future.

Prologue

In the Beginning

A young mendicant showed up at the Munjal family home in the summer of 1932. He was nine or ten years old, with a shaven head and clad only in a *dhoti*[1]. There was a sacred thread across his skinny chest. He demanded alms, as if it were his birthright.

Indeed it was. The lad's name was Brijmohan and he had come home. Two years earlier, he had run away to join a *gurukul*, or school of Vedic learning. There, he studied the tenets of Vedic philosophy and learned to recite and interpret *shlokas* (verses) from the scriptures. When his mother insisted that he come home, he finally agreed to return, but asked for *bhiksha* (traditional alms), in keeping with his status as a *brahmachari* (a celibate).

---

1 A garment worn by male Hindus, consisting of a plain piece of fabric tied around the waist and extending to cover most of the legs.

This *gurukul* lay on the outskirts of Kamalia, an ancient town in the plains of western Punjab (now in Pakistan) and home to the Munjal clan. The town boasted just one school on the British pattern and it was here that the wool merchant Bahadur Chand Munjal, conscious that a 'modern' education was fast becoming an imperative in British India, had enrolled his sons.

However, the fourth of his six sons, Satyanand, had chosen to attend the *gurukul*. The *Arya Samaj*[2], having broken with orthodox Hinduism, had set up Vedic schools to offer Indians an alternative to the British model of education. The spiritual rigour and discipline of the *gurukul* appealed to Satyanand's ascetic nature. Young Brijmohan, who adored his older sibling and followed him in many things, wanted to attend the *gurukul* as well. His frugality, spiritual bent and desire to explore his inner self all pointed him in that direction. Yet he had not been able to muster up the courage to tell his parents of his compulsive desire to join the *gurukul*.

One morning, Brijmohan vanished. Brimming with daring and determination, the lad arrived at the *gurukul* and demanded admission. So impressed were the teachers with his enterprise and commitment that they accepted him on the spot. At barely eight years of age, Brijmohan had embarked on a mission of self-discovery.

He fitted seamlessly into his new environs and began to focus his energies on imbibing the religious texts and life skills, while simultaneously strengthening his inner awareness. Brijmohan had become a proper little *brahmachari*.

When his mother learnt of his whereabouts, she had mixed feelings; she was relieved that he was safe and sound, but perturbed about the path he had chosen. At the same time, she realized she had no choice in the matter. An *acharya*[3] consoled her: 'Don't look at

[2] A Hindu reform movement founded by Maharishi Dayanand Saraswati, in 1875. The followers of *Arya Samaj* are against idol-worship and meaningless rituals in modern Hinduism, and aim to return to the Vedas in their beliefs and ritual.

[3] In Indian culture, an *acharya* is a Brahmin head guide or instructor in religious matters.

him as an eight-year-old; he has a fire within that will take him very far one day.'

* *

That's the first-ever story I heard about my father. It was recounted as an example of the steely resolve and fortitude he displayed even as a young boy. To me, it explained something else: my father's life-long detachment from all wordly things. It wasn't that he could never own luxuries; just that they never owned him. There's no better way of explaining the paradox of a man who built a billion-dollar empire and yet, prefered the lifestyle of a simple middle class man.

He stayed at the *gurukul* for two years; head shaven, clad in a *dhoti*, with a *yagyopaveet* (multi stranded sacred cotton thread) bisecting his chest and Sanskrit shlokas on his lips. All his life, he would recount incidents and learnings from the *gurukul*. He learnt to steer his own course early on and grew up to become – as his family and friends would say – a forceful personality.

My grandmother had strong reservations about surrendering not one, but two of her sons to the *gurukul*. What if they preferred to stay back at the ashram, instead of returning home? She was not prepared to let her younger son remain at the ashram, indefinitely. Sensing her apprehension, my father made no protest when she insisted on his return. Fearful that he might try to go back, my grandmother shoved him into a room and locked the door, determined to never let him go again.

My grandfather was delighted at his return, because he wanted his younger sons to complete their formal schooling and find jobs like their older brothers. Brijmohan, still rooted in the values of the *gurukul*, understood he would have to approach the world on different terms. That epiphany altered the course of his life. 'He (my grandfather) sowed the seeds of a change in my thinking,' my father often recalled.

The realization was a simple one. His place, now and for always, was with his family.

* *

It all began in the early years of the twentieth century, when Thakuri Devi (my grandmother) married Bahadur Chand Munjal (my grandfather). The couple was blessed with seven sons and a daughter, Santosh Kumari. The eldest, Bal Mukund, was quickly followed by Sadanand, Dayanand, Satyanand, Sohan Lal, Brijmohan Lall and Om Prakash. Sohan Lal passed away quite young and it was the seven siblings who grew up together.

In 1923, the year my father was born, Kamalia was a peaceful town in the prosperous Lyallpur district of Punjab (later Faislabad and, now, Toba Tek Singh district). Situated a few kilometres away from the banks of the river Ravi and about 185 km from Lahore, its mixed population of Hindus and Muslims numbered less than 20,000. The 'Pakistan Declaration' (authored by Choudhary Rahmat Ali in 1933) was still in the future and the serrated saw of Partition had not yet been conceived.

The town had existed at least as far back as 325 BC, when Alexander the Great rampaged through it during his campaign against the Malli tribe. Historically, it was known as 'Kot' (Fort) Kamalia, a reference to the wall constructed around it by Raja Sircup Singh in fourth century CE. (Legend has it that he was a rather fierce chap, with a penchant for playing polo with the heads of his opponents.)

Kamalia may have derived its modern name during the time of Ibrahim Lodhi, when Sircup's city was handed over to Kamal Khan, but historians remain divided on the issue. The town boasts a Jehangiri Mosque dating back (as the name suggests) to the reign of Mughal Emperor Jehangir. During the 1857 revolt, it was the site of a popular uprising. The townspeople held out against the British for a week – no small feat, to my mind.

Towards the end of the nineteenth century, a railhead had reached the town and trade began to prosper. The British also developed a canal system on the river, turning it into one of the most fertile agricultural belts in the state. This was particularly true of the eastern part of the district, where crop cultivation flourished – primarily wheat, sugarcane, rice and cotton. The British administration began allotting land to farmers, which attracted people from other parts of the province (mainly from Lahore, Jalandhar and Hoshiarpur). Agri-based enterprises, like cotton-ginning units, spinning mills and sugar mills, sprang up.

Kamalia became an important agricultural hub and textile centre, manufacturing both mill-made and traditional handmade cloth, particularly *khaddar* (a homespun cotton cloth) and carpets. Two big markets – Sadar Bazaar and Iqbal Bazaar – came up, dealing with agricultural produce and finished goods.

My forebearers were 'Aroravanshis' – an intermediate caste between *kshatriya* (warrior) and *vaishya* (merchants) though these distinctions of caste were never made in our family – Aroravanshis were engaged in the raw wool trade in the early 1900s. My grandfather, Bahadur Chand, his elder brother Ganga Ram and his cousin, Kishan Singh, sourced raw wool from farmers in the area, who bred sheep in their regions.

As Kamalia gained in importance as a centre for trade in agricultural commodities, my grandfather began dealing in foodgrains. He opened a small wholesale shop. Gradually, his business expanded and he became an important supplier. Known for his ethical business practices, he commanded the respect of not just the trading community but also the farmers who supplied him goods, as they knew they would always get a fair price. Buyers trusted him, because his goods were never adulterated and he did not indulge in price manipulation or hoarding.

Bahadur Chand's sons imbibed these lessons in honesty, which became integral to their business philosophy in the years to come. Uncle Om Prakash often repeated what his father had told him and his brothers: 'If you make honesty your business, you will prosper in any business you take up.'

By all accounts, the Munjals were a happy family. My grandfather was a gentle, soft-spoken and hardworking man. My grandmother looked after the home and hearth and deftly balanced the household budget. 'In those days, money was very limited, but my mother managed the house skilfully and cheerfully. She made it her priority to pay off the family dues, despite our own hardships. This left a deep impression on me and I imbibed this practice in my business,' my father would recall.

Meticulous in matters of finance, she also had an altruistic streak and was ever willing to help those in need. 'If someone was ill and needed attention, she was there. If someone was planning a celebration and needed a hand with the arrangements, she would oblige,' uncle Om Prakash would often reminisce. My father inherited his sociability from her. He also learnt to regard philanthropy as a social obligation.

The family's day would start with a *havan*, the Vedic ritual promoted by the *Arya Samaj*. Like all members of the Samaj, my grandparents were strict vegetarians. My grandmother followed a tradition common among Hindus and Sikhs in undivided Punjab in those days; before every meal, the first roti would be broken and one part offered to a cow, another to a dog and the third to the birds. Only then would the family sit down to eat. This ritual was based on the belief that all living creatures are entitled to a share of the earth's bounty.

My grandmother also subscribed to the *Guru Granth Sahib* (the sacred text of the Sikhs, regarded as the eternal living guru). She would perform *kar sewa* (service) at the gurdwara (Sikh temple) every morning by sweeping and swabbing the floors. The Munjal brothers were exposed to both traditions.

Like many families, the Munjals had their brush with tragedies. Sohan Lal, who was born just before my father, was killed in an accident at the age of seven. It took every ounce of my grandmother's resilience to get over it, but recover she did and never allowed the loss to diminish her outgoing and generous nature.

A major factor responsible for maintaining family harmony was my mother and grandmother's insistence on respecting elders. This was non-negotiable. Not only was it incumbent upon all the children to respect their parents, but the younger ones were expected to defer to their older brothers, who in turn, would look after them. This habit stayed with them through their lives; my father would touch his older brothers' feet every time they met, even if it was three times in a day.

Uncle Om Prakash made it a practice to press his mother's legs each evening, to alleviate the fatigue of her action-packed day, so that she could find the energy to do what she enjoyed most, which was to spend time amongst people.

My grandfather's legendary honesty stood the test of adversity. During Partition, when normal life and commerce had been disrupted, food was scarce. The brothers managed to find a packet of food in an abandoned building and brought it home for the family to share. Bahadur Chand asked them where they had found it. When they told him, he instructed them to take it back as someone must have gathered the food, perhaps at great risk, for his own family and stashed it away. He told his sons it was wrong of them to fill their stomachs at another's expense. Abashed, the brothers returned the packet of food and the family went hungry that day.

* *

The Munjal brothers grew up in a time of great economic and political turmoil. The rising tide of nationalism was gaining strength across India, even as the common man laboured under the double burden of poverty and unemployment. By the time my father reached his teens, in the mid-1930s, India was reeling under the impact of the Great Depression of 1929.

While Western historians have argued that the fallout on India was marginal, it must be remembered that the slowdown was coupled with the restrictive policies of the British Raj. A protective trade policy proved beneficial to the United Kingdom, but damaged the Indian economy. Between 1929 and 1937, exports and imports fell drastically. The agricultural sector, in particular, was severely affected.

Markets for Indian goods vanished, leaving small-scale manufacturers and farmers who had shifted from food to cash crops, in the lurch. The jute industry was a case in point; world demand fell and prices plunged. Indian exports were halved between 1929 and 1932, even as the British Raj refused to consider ameliorative steps, such as devaluation of the Indian currency or increase in government expenditure.

At the same time, imports also fell by 47 per cent. The Swadeshi movement had picked up steam in the 1920s and curtailed consumption of foreign goods. The cumulative effect of the export and import crunch was acutely felt by the Railways, which suffered a massive drop in freight traffic. Seaborne international trade, too, was crippled.

The common man was devastated by the increase in domestic prices of commodities, in tandem with stringent taxation. Cash was hard to come by. The political repercussions were as profound as they were inevitable. Farmers rebelled and the freedom struggle picked up steam, manifesting itself through movements such as Civil Disobedience and the Salt Satyagraha of 1930.

Against this backdrop of pervasive economic hardship, Bahadur Chand Munjal's sons found it difficult to continue with their education, and it became imperative to supplement the family income as quickly as possible. On the other hand, joining their father's business was not an option; it just wasn't big enough. So the sons opted to find jobs as soon as they could. Yet other than farming and trade, the town had little to offer by way of occupation. It was not surprising, therefore, that my father's first job in 1938 was on a farm as a 15-year old.

The job involved my father parking himself at the sugar cane fields while the harvest was underway and counting the number of sugar cane bundles being loaded for transportation to the market. It was gruelling work, physically and mentally, because he had to stand throughout the day and remain alert. At sunset, each evening he would narrate the figures to the munim (accountant).

His hard work and integrity (which ensured that no bundles were unaccounted for), endeared him to his supervisor. What's more, he cheerfully accepted any and all tasks assigned to him and discharged them with aplomb. He became a favourite of his employer. He worked in the fields for around five years, but the family and my father himself realized that he was capable of much more. His talents clearly demanded a larger canvas, but where?

The answer lay to the west, in Quetta, not far from the Afghanistan border (around 150 km). My father's older brothers – uncles Sadanand, Dayanand and Satyanand – were already working in Quetta (which means 'fort' in the Pashto tongue).

* *

My father's elder brother, uncle Dayanand, had been the first to reach Quetta. He completed his schooling in 1931 and went to Quetta in 1933. The bustling town was the capital of the Baluchistan province and often referred to as a 'mini-London' because it was dotted with multi-storey buildings.

The British had occupied Quetta in 1876 and turned it into an important strategic, marketing and communications centre. The town grew around the Residency (founded by Sir Robert Sandeman) and its strongly garrisoned army station. By 1896, it had its own municipality. The Army Command and Staff College came up in 1907. Several army depots also mushroomed.

Quetta was the starting point of the trade corridor into Afghanistan and was also famous for its orchards and dry fruit marts, which earned it the sobriquet 'Fruit Garden'. There were jobs aplenty and people from all over (then undivided) India, flocked there in droves looking for work. Brijmohan's brothers were among them. Job opportunities were scarce in their hometown but in Quetta, some of them found work at the ordnance factory.

Catastrophe was, however, round the corner. A massive earthquake, measuring 7.7 on the Richter scale, struck the region in the early hours of 31 May 1935. It was 3.40 a.m. and most people were still asleep. The earthquake lasted for about three minutes and the tremors were felt as far as Agra. When the tremors stopped, buildings were razed to rubble and 20,000 people lay dead in Quetta alone.

An official government release from Shimla stated:

> The whole city of Quetta is destroyed ... it is estimated that 20,000 corpses remain buried under the debris. There is no hope of rescuing any more persons alive. The corpses extracted and buried number several thousand. There are about 10,000 Indian survivors including 4,000 injured. All houses in the civil area are razed to the ground except Government House, which is partially standing but in ruins. The church and club are both in ruins, also the Murree Brewery. One quarter of the cantonment area is destroyed, the remaining three quarters slightly damaged but inhabitable. Most of the damage was done in the RAF area where the barracks were destroyed and only six out of the twenty-seven machines are serviceable. The railway area is destroyed. Hanna Road and the Staff College are undamaged. Surrounding villages are destroyed with, it is feared, very heavy casualties. All the villages between Quetta and Khelat are also reported to have been destroyed.

Loss to life and property was huge. The death toll in the region was estimated at 20,000–60,000. Among the survivors, half of whom were seriously injured, were the Munjal brothers. Uncles Sadanand and Satyanand escaped unscathed but uncle Dayanand was less fortunate.

The building in which they lived collapsed and while uncle Satyanand managed to escape, uncle Dayanand was buried under the rubble. After thirty-six hours, he was somehow taken out alive. Uncle Dayanand's back was permanently damaged-recovery was slow and painful, and the family suffered with him. He would endure a measure of pain and walked bent over for the rest of his life. In fact, uncle Dayanand would prove unlucky in terms of accidents even in the future. Soon after the first Hero factory came up on 26 April 1958, a large number of steel sheets came crashing down on him and he broke his thigh in several places.

Quetta recovered, too. My uncles went back to work and encouraged my father to apply for a job there. The snag was that all the openings were for office-oriented clerical jobs and my father was unsure of his chances of getting one. His brothers were mechanics and family discussions usually revolved around physical work rather than office roles. No one in the family had ever held a white collar job before.

To his surprise, the ordnance factory responded to his application and selected him for a clerk's position. At the age of twenty, he had managed to get the most prestigious job in the family. My father learnt an important lesson that stayed with him for the rest of his life: even if you believe you're not capable, seize the opportunity because it may well reveal a completely new side of yourself. And when you take a risk, you push yourself harder to succeed.

To dream beyond your means takes imagination and courage. My father had both; throughout his life, people would tell him he was overreaching, but he would remain undeterred.

Uncle Satyanand recalled: 'Such a lucky chap! We were all on daily wages. He started on a monthly salary. It was very rare in those days.'

My cousin, Vijay, uncle Dayanand's son, recalls the tough grind as narrated by his father:

> My father Dayanandji – who went on to found Hero along with my uncles that later became a global leader, started humbly. He found work as a daily wage worker at the ordnance factory and was paid ₹1.50 per day, till his salary was gradually regularized to ₹165 per month (which gave him the confidence to get married in December 1938!). He worked in Quetta till January 1942, and then left for Ferozepur and worked at the army canteen store where he earned only ₹4 per day.

* *

My father immersed himself in his new workplace. The fact that he faced a vertical learning curve excited him, because it gave him an opportunity to prove himself. As my brother Suman says, '*Unhone apna bhi kaam karna aur baakiyon ka bhi*' (he would do his own work and take on the work of others, too).

My father's supervisor was impressed with his organizational ability, which was reflected in his daily to-do lists. In time, his talents and ability to finish chores ahead of time, came to the attention of the British officers posted at the ordnance factory. In pre-Partition India, the British were still at the helm of affairs and their approval was a prerequisite for making progress.

News of my father's resourcefulness and enterprise spread up the ladder of the official hierarchy and a series of rapid promotions resulted. He bypassed his peers and a stellar career appeared to be in store for him. My father always stressed on the importance of his stint at the ordnance factory. He said: '(It) provided me with my first English lessons; from them (the British) I also learnt the importance of discipline at the workplace. I learnt about punctuality. I learnt about commitment and the importance of doing the job at hand. I also learnt the basics of managing logistics and materials.'

One morning, he arrived at the factory to find the doors shut. He had reached at 8.01 a.m. instead of 8.00 a.m., just one minute past the clock, but he was not allowed in and missed a whole day of work. He was never late again. That lesson on the value of time remained with him. All his life, he never took his own or anyone else's time for granted.

The most important thing he and his siblings learnt, however, was the care and maintenance of bicycles. The ordnance factory imparted training in two kinds of machinery, which prima facie appeared to have nothing to do with each other: guns and bicycles. The latter, I assume, were valuable to the war effort from the communications point of view. The skills the brothers picked up in Quetta would alter the course of their lives, but of course, they did not know it at the time.

The capacity for hard work was a trait shared by all the Munjal brothers. Despite the tough weather conditions in Quetta, they were always the first ones to arrive at work and the last to leave. My mother recalled hearing stories of their gruelling lifestyle: 'In Quetta, Sadanand, Dayanand and Brijmohan worked at the army factory till 8 p.m., when the gates shut. To reach home, they had to trek through deep drifts of snow.'

During this phase of his life, my father discovered an aspect of his personality that stood him in good stead in later years – the ability to make friends and keep them for life. In the *Book of Letters* that we (the Munjal family) brought out to commemorate my father's ninetieth birthday, almost every page reflected the relationships he had nurtured. Nothing was more valuable to him, or more quintessentially human, than to make and maintain connections based on mutual affection.

Sometimes, the investments in friendships called for great sacrifice. One morning, while working at his desk in the ordnance depot, my father heard that a close friend's father was critically ill. Bikramjit Mehta was a childhood buddy and my father had spent many pleasurable hours at his home in Pathankot. He knew the whole family very well. When he heard of uncle Mehta's illness, he immediately asked for leave. His boss was not inclined to grant his request, but my father was adamant and got his way.

In Pathankot, he found that Bikramjit's father's health had deteriorated. He proved a pillar of strength for the Mehta family. His leave was exhausted, but Bikramjit's father was no better. My father knew that in all conscience, he could not leave his friend's side. He sent a telegram to his superiors, requesting an extension of his leave. His boss categorically refused and indicated that his service would be terminated unless he returned to his post immediately. My father did not think twice. He stayed on at Pathankot, lost his job, and when his friend no longer needed him returned to Kamalia without regrets.

All his life, even in business, my father would prioritize relationships over pragmatism. He never drew a line between 'business' and 'the personal'. Uncle Om Prakash, his junior by five years, imbibed this philosophy as well. The brothers' beliefs were rooted in the cultural milieu from which they had sprung. The emphasis on family ties and a sense of *apnapan* or belonging was at odds with the contractual style of management popularized by the West. It became the basis of the Munjals' work culture and was one of the attributes that prompted Japanese auto major Honda to partner with us decades later.

My father's early grounding in the ancient Indian texts may have helped shape his business outlook. The values of truth, trust and social responsibility informed his decisions and became the cornerstone of his legacy. In subsequent chapters, I will try and explain his uniquely indigenous business *dharma*.

* *

Uncle Satyanand was among the first of the Munjal brothers to deploy the mechanical skills he had learned in Quetta in a private enterprise. As mentioned earlier, his early education took place at the same *gurukul* that my father later joined. There he acquired a wide knowledge of Sanskrit, the Vedas and the *samskaras* (traditions), which formed the basis of his entire philosophy of life.

When he managed factory operations, his calm and reassuring demeanour drew co-workers to him. His frugality, maturity and nobility was such that friends and relatives began to rely on him for advice and guidance. In later years, the *Arya Samaj* acknowledged his commitment to its social service programmes by conferring on him the title of 'Mahatma' (a revered person regarded with love and respect, and also seen as a person of faith), a moniker that was quickly adopted by many who knew him.

After school, uncle Satyanand followed the same trajectory as his older brothers, working at the ordnance factory in Quetta. His older brothers persuaded him to apply for recruitment to the army, but he flunked the interview because he was flat-footed. Perhaps it was fortuitous, because had he joined, his brothers would have certainly followed him; and the four youngsters from Kamalia who actually went, lost their lives in the Second World War.

After uncle Satyanand returned from Quetta, he briefly joined his elder brother Bal Mukund, who was involved in coal trading, before uncle Dayanand asked him to go to Lahore, where a friend ran a bicycle shop. Uncle Satyanand agreed and began handling purchases, besides learning how to repair punctures.

The job at Lahore suited uncle Satyanand. He had no desire to move to another city for a government job and seized the opportunity to learn about the new industry.

He quickly became invaluable to his employer. In a matter of a month, the proprietor entrusted the shop to uncle Satyanand and focused his attention on bringing in new business. Uncle Satyanand encouraged him to diversify. Bolstered by his confidence in uncle Satyanand's judgement, the proprietor began retailing sewing machines. Marketing a new product aimed at housewives and involving a substantive investment wasn't easy. To attract customers, he offered after-sales service and repair.

Uncle Satyanand now applied his formidable mechanical skills to sewing machines. He had a fine eye for detail and understood the nuts and bolts of both machines so well that he could have built a bicycle or a sewing machine from scratch.

It was in Lahore, so I am told, that my uncle met my aunt, Pushpa Devi and married her. Family ties proved too strong for him and he eventually moved back to Kamalia. He brought with him his first-born son, Yogesh, who was admitted into a local school.

Uncle Dayanand, too, got involved in the bicycle business. My cousin Vijay managed to dig out an old diary, in which his father had meticulously jotted down all the major milestones in his life.

From Quetta, uncle Dayanand wrote, he went to Ferozepur, where he worked until September 1943. In January 1944, he joined my uncles Sadanand and Satyanand who had set up a bicycle parts business in Amritsar. Uncle Om Prakash joined his elder brothers just around Partition.

In 1946, there were massive floods in Amritsar; ironically, also around this time, the bicycle parts store got burgled, and my uncles traced the thief to Agra. Sadanandji and Satyanandji followed him there, managed to recover most of the stolen goods, and decided to set up base in Agra itself. Dayanandji, however, preferred to go to Ludhiana, where he was joined later by Om Prakashji. They opened a small bicycle trading business. They began visiting bicycle parts shops and asking for their requirements, and then took their orders to supply shops. They acted as middlemen and retained some commission. They eventually earned enough to start their own shop. As their business grew, they began to experience a shortage of parts supplies and decided to manufacture one part on their own, the top portion of a bicycle fork. Eventually they acquired a workshop and began manufacturing the entire fork and soon, added more parts as they gained confidence. While Dayanandji manned the workshed, Om Prakashji travelled to various cities as a salesman, trying to convince dealers to sell the parts they were making. They continued to do this till the government allowed bicycle makers to manufacture on a large scale. Following this, the first Hero Cycles factory came up in 1956 at Miller Ganj near Viswakarma Chowk.

* *

The bicycle industry had made a low-profile debut in India in the early years of the twentieth century. Like any machine with moving parts, the bicycle was subject to breakdown and needed repair from time to time. Bicycle parts were largely imported but small units manufacturing replacement parts came up in Calcutta (now Kolkata) before World War I and, by the 1930s, began popping up in other parts of the country. The brothers had entered the business at the right time, when it was poised for growth.

Back in Kamalia, using some of the money he earned from the cycle business, Satyanand had started renovating the family home. Everyone advised him against it, because the winds of change were in the air, but he paid no heed. Yogesh says that his *Naniji* (mother's mother) travelled all the way from Montgomery to dissuade him, but to no avail. The Kamalia home grew bigger, and at the time of the Partition, only the plastering of the house remained.

1

Winds of Change

At the age of twenty-four, my father got a second shot at life. He was standing on the roof of a friend's home in Kamalia, when he came within a hair's breadth of life. A communal riot had broken out, one of the many that marked the Partition of India. As he watched the bloodletting and acts of arson, to the accompaniment of screams and gunfire, a red-hot pain seared across his forehead.

He clapped a hand over his brow and it came away bloody. A stray bullet had ploughed a furrow just above his right eyebrow. A centimetre either side and it could have been fatal. He placed his hand over the injury, the wound forgotten in the greater pain of watching his country bleed. Independent India would carry the scar of the communal riots. So would my father, Brijmohan Lall Munjal.

If someone had told him in 1940 that his country would be torn apart and the province of Punjab divided, my father would not have believed it. In March of that year, the Lahore Resolution had called for an independent Muslim state. Seven years earlier, Choudhary Rahmat Ali had coined the term 'Pakstan' (the 'i' was added later). Still, no one in Kamalia could have conjured a reality where their town, an hour's drive from Harappa (one of the most famous archaeological sites in the world), would become part of a whole new country.

So unfathomable was the idea of migrating from Lyallpur even in the mid-1940s that uncle Satyanand decided to renovate the ancestral home. Yet as the construction progressed, he became preoccupied with another family matter.

My father, who had turned twenty-five, had shown himself capable of getting a good job and thus his prospects as a worthy groom were bright. Uncle Satyanand felt it was time his gifted young brother started a family of his own and began scouting for a suitable match. He deployed his wife's family connections in Lahore for the purpose. They passed the word around. One of them happened to mention the eligible Munjal bachelor to a relative, who was working with an insurance company.[4] It turned out that this gentleman's wife had an unmarried sister, Santosh, who was petite and pretty and from an unexceptionable background. Her father was a doctor, fortuitously at Samundri, around 50 kilometres from Kamalia, and Tara Chand, my *maasi's* (mother's sister) husband, lost no time in finalizing the match.

So, in the penultimate years of the world's largest freedom struggle, with hostilities between communities sharpening and dire winds pregnant with violence, change and displacement, blowing across the country, two young people found themselves engaged.

* *

---

4 The link with insurance continued within their family and his son, Mohan Mehta managed insurance policies for our family members for a long time.

In remote Kamalia, there were heated discussions, protests in the streets and communal tension. It was a reflection of the atmosphere in the country, gripped alike by nationalistic fervour and distrust between Hindus and Muslims.

It was clear that the British had lost their hold over India, even as the Second World War raged on. The British parliament sent a delegation led by Sir Stafford Cripps to secure Indian support for the war effort in 1942. The Indian National Congress, led by Mahatma Gandhi, rejected the British offer of a new constitution and dominion status (instead of full independence) for India after the war. The Muslim League also cold-shouldered the offer, but for different reasons.

The Congress responded to the failure of the Cripps Mission by launching the Quit India movement. In a stirring speech on 8 August 1942, at the Gowalia Tank Maidan in Bombay, half a kilometre away from Gokuldas Tejpal Sanskrit College, where the Indian National Congress had been founded more than half a century earlier, Mahatma Gandhi called for 'determined, passive resistance'.

'Here is a mantra, a short one that I give you,' he said. 'You may imprint it on your hearts and let every breath of yours give expression to it. The mantra is: Do or Die.'

The Mahatma's 'do or die' call reached every corner of the country and became a rallying cry for all Indians. The Quit India movement took off on the following day. Gandhi and most of the top Congress leadership were arrested, leaving the movement rudderless.

The political turbulence had an economic context. The Second World War had adversely affected the Indian economy. In the first few months after the war broke out, exports rose on a demand for agricultural commodities but soon encountered shipping difficulties, as one country after another fell to Germany in the west and Japan in the east.

India's trade fell by a factor of one-sixth, mainly on account of groundnuts, raw jute and oilseeds, resulting in a surplus of these commodities on one hand and shortage of foodgrains on the other.

Indeed, the exigencies of war put tremendous pressure on food supplies, thanks to the increased presence of soldiers, war evacuees and prisoners. At the same time, the marketable surplus declined, with farmers preferring to hold on to their produce. Imports fell sharply, from 2.15 million tonnes in 1939 to just 0.5 million tonnes in 1941. Stockpiling was encouraged by fears of currency depreciation and the expectation of a further rise in prices.

Food crops in Bengal had already been impacted by a series of natural disasters. To make matters worse, the supply of Burmese rice to Bengal was cut off when Rangoon (now Yangon) fell to Japan in April 1942. The massive influx of refugees from Burma put further strain on food stocks. Addding fuel to the fire, the British followed 'scorched earth' and 'denial policies'. To impede a possible invasion of India through Burma, they chose to remove or destroy stocks of paddy (unmilled rice) in south Bengal rather than allow them to fall into Japanese hands. Compounding the shortage was the diversion of food supplies to the military.

The British-Indian administration failed miserably to free up foodgrain stocks and ensure their equitable distribution. Landlords with large surpluses benefitted from the rise in prices of agricultural commodities but small farmers and agricultural labourers suffered. Many were forced to sell their lands in order to survive. In 1943–44, an estimated 25 per cent of small farmers were alienated from their land.

It was a perfect storm of adversity: war, natural disasters and administrative incompetence of stunning proportions. The result was the Bengal Famine of 1943. Cholera, dysentery, malaria and small pox stalked a starved population, wiping out millions in present-day West Bengal, Odisha, Bihar and Bangladesh.

The Munjal family followed the news of war and famine with consternation. Little did they know that the horror of mass starvation would soon be followed by the traumatic ordeal of Partition.

It was my father who first realized that the unthinkable had become the inevitable. One morning, he was at his teak bureau, at the family home in Kamalia, attending to paperwork while listening to the news on the radio. It was all about the talks being held on Partition. Muhammad Ali Jinnah, the leader of the Muslim League, was adamant, despite the Mahatma's pleas.

All at once, my father put down his pen and gazed out of the window, deep in thought. Framed by the window, he saw his indefatigable elder brother hard at work, orchestrating the remodelling of the family home. His mind's eye turned towards the north-east, leapt across the Ravi and 200 km of fields, to Amritsar. He wondered whether the border would be drawn there, when the country was divided?

Even in his early twenties, my father was mature beyond his years. He had learnt to trust his instincts, which were now telling him that the family's cosy existence in Kamalia was fast approaching an end. It would be an awful wrench, but if they were to survive, they would have to uproot themselves from the land of their forefathers and make a fresh start elsewhere. He was to be married soon; he must secure his wife's future and help the family as well.

My father recalled approaching the family elders with the idea. He would later say: 'Our father told us to figure out the way forward ourselves ... some members of the family refused to believe that Partition was actually going to happen even though we were already beginning to see fights and skirmishes all around us.'

So a family meeting was called and they huddled together as my father described, point by point, the information emanating from news bulletins. He said it was time to face the truth, appalling though it seemed. Partition was no longer a remote possibility, but a strong probability. The family must plan for the future, if they were to have one at all.

It was apparent that Amritsar would remain in India. Two of the brothers, uncles Sadanand and Satyanand decided to go there and set up a business, so that when Partition occurred and they needed to leave Kamalia in a hurry, the family would have a source of livelihood.

The choice of business was governed by fate and expediency. The war that had impacted Bengal so horribly, had proved beneficial to Indian industry. Large government orders fuelled the growth of industries old and new. Among the old, cement, cotton textiles, iron and steel and sugar expanded substantially. For instance, the production of cement and paper increased by 96 per cent between 1937–1945, while textiles grew by 20 per cent and steel by 43 per cent. The overall index of profits (base 1928) rose from 72 in 1939, to 163 in 1945.

Among the newly burgeoning industries were diesel engines, pumps, sewing machines, machine tools, and bicycles.

The Munjal brothers knew bicycles. They did not have any capital, but possessed the technical knowledge and skills to make their mark in the rapidly growing bicycle industry.

Just around Partition, teen-aged Om Prakashji joined his elder brothers, who had set up a shop in Amritsar in 1944. Uncle Om Prakash described in his typical raconteur style the atmosphere of the time: '*Jung chal rahi thi* (the war was on) ... *bada chhota kaam tha* (it was not grand at all, the work) ... cycle parts *ka* (of cycle parts). It was war time, imported parts were not arriving. Indian-made parts were found in Amritsar and Ludhiana. These were very big markets which supplied all over India. We started trading in cycle parts by procuring them from the market.'

My father would add to the narrative: 'On the road, there were nothing other than bicycles and when they broke down, there were virtually no spares available. Some artisans in Ludhiana, Malerkotla, Sialkot, Amritsar and Lahore started making components in a very crude way. People like us would find imported parts and bring these to those artisans and give them some money to re-engineer them.'

Uncle Dayanand told us that even though my father was in Kamalia at the time the cycle parts shop was started, he did his bit to help the fledgling business in Amritsar that he and my other elder uncles were managing. I still remember the deep affection reflected in his eyes when he narrated the story of my father's very first business coup: 'Brijmohan went all the way to Quetta and came back with a ₹2,500 order. It was the biggest order we had ever received.' In those days, this was a king's ransom for a small business.

✻ ✻

When the Second World War came to a close, it was obvious that the independence of India would soon follow. The prospect intensified rather than lessened the conflicts between the Congress and Muslim League. The Shimla Conference of 1945 (called by the Governor General, Lord Archibald Wavell) and members of the Cabinet Mission of 1946 (despatched by British Prime Minister Clement Atlee) failed to resolve their differences.

On 16 August 1946, the Muslim League announced 'Direct Action' to press its demand for a separate homeland for Muslims. Communal tension erupted in Calcutta and spilled over to Noakhali and other parts of Bengal, gradually spreading to Bihar and the United Provinces and, finally, to Punjab.

From early 1947 onwards, the Munjals heard reports of riots, looting and arson from all over the as yet undivided province: Ferozepur, Ludhiana, Jalandhar, Gurdaspur, Sialkot, Rawalpindi, Lahore, Amritsar, Montgomery and their own home district, Lyallpur. All three communities in Punjab had their own militias and the violence appeared to be systematic. Hindus and Sikhs were being targeted in Muslim-dominated west Punjab. It was the other way around in east Punjab. Between March and May of that year, there were 3,600 riot-related deaths in the province, according to official figures.

✻ ✻

The Mountbatten Plan of 3 June 1947 accepted the principle of Partition and recognized the fully sovereign nations of India and Pakistan. Now, it only remained for Cyril Radcliffe, the chairman of the Boundary Commission, to demarcate the two nations. The Munjals waited with bated breath for his verdict. Would Amritsar, where Dayanand and Om Prakash had set up shop, go to India as they had anticipated?

Radcliffe, who arrived in India only in July and therefore had barely five weeks to complete the job (by August 15), drew his famous line through Attari, midway between Lahore and Amritsar.

Even after the line was drawn, the Sikhs and Hindus were reluctant to leave the fertile lands of Lyallpur district and with good reason as it was the richest tract in the entire province. Plus, they had also invested heavily in industry. Hoping against hope that they would be assured of security, they vacillated. To quote Gurcharan Das, author and former CEO of Procter & Gamble India 'Lyallpur was a prosperous district where most of the capital was invested in cotton ginning, weaving, flour and sugar mills.The Hindus of Lyallpur thus lingered on, desperately hoping that this madness would pass and peace would soon return.'[5]

It was clear that Hindus and Sikhs were unwelcome in the new nation. Despite the assurances and efforts of the Deputy Commissoner of Lyallpur, a certain Mr Hamid, violence erupted in Tandlianwala (some 90 km from Kamalia) in late August, where a gurdwara was razed and many Sikhs were killed.

A few days later, Kamalia became the scene of a bloody riot. On 1 September, the Hindu military in the town had been replaced by Muslim troops and the following week, a Muslim mob went on a rampage. Rumour had it that the violence was incited by Muslim soldiers who arrived in Kamalia on a refugee train. Whatever the reason, mob fury was directed against Hindu and Sikh establishments, places of worship and schools. The Khalsa High School, where the brothers had studied, and the Arya Putri Pathshala were attacked. Many people were killed and dozens of young girls were abducted. It was only when a prominent *zamindar* (landlord), Nawab Sadat Ali Khan, appealed to the mob with folded hands that the violence stopped.

At this time Francis Mudie, the governor of west Punjab, arrived in Lyallpur and was keen to ensure that the non-Muslim population of

[5] Gurcharan Das, *A Fine Family* (India: Penguin, 1990)

the district moved out peacefully. In a letter to Mr Jinnah, he wrote: 'There is still little sign of the three lakh (one lakh equals 100,000) Sikhs in Lyallpur moving, but in the end they too will have to go.' He now directed the district commissioner to move them to a refugee camp prior to evacuation. However, those who sought to leave risked death, and in mid-September, a foot convoy from Kamalia was attacked, slaughtering nine.

The Munjals heard of families being hustled to the evacuation camps and large convoys – as many as 400,000 strong – leaving Montgomery and Lyallpur for Ferozepur. Landlords, shopkeepers, doctors, labourers, artisans – all kinds of people – funnelled into India via the Lyallpur–Balloki–Chunian–Ferozepur road. An estimated 50–60,000 evacuees poured into Ferozepur on a daily basis. Within a week of Independence, a million refugees crossed from west to east Punjab and in the following week, another 2.5 million gathered in the refugee camps.

From all over the district – Gojra, Toba Tek Singh, Arauti, Samundri – came news of massacres, mass rape and pillaging, often with the participation of the military. At the refugee camp at Tandlianwala, 115 Hindus and Sikhs were killed in an attack. A convoy was stopped at a railway crossing in Lyallpur town and massacred. Another convoy of 5,000 from Lyallpur, escorted by the military, was attacked by a mob at Baloki Head (75 km from Lahore) and 1,000 refugees were killed.[6]

Violence intensified and the evacuation took on a fresh urgency. Stories of abduction, rape and mutilation of women on both sides of the border made it imperative to flee. A particularly moving story inolved a truck convoy that rolled into Lyallpur, carrying a number of young women who had been waylaid short of Lahore and brutalized by a mob.

---

6 https://archive.org/details/in.ernet.dli.2015.99365/page/n199 (*Stern Reckoning* by Gopal Das Khosla, first published 1949, pg 165-172)

The Munjal family, like all the Hindus in the region, had to run for their lives. Somehow, uncle Satyanand escorted his still fledgling family, including my father and grandparents, out of town. They took the last bus out of Kamalia to Amritsar. My mother, Santosh, also made her way to India with her parents via a train. Yogesh, who was very young at the time, still remembers the 'many mishappenings' he saw during the journey.

The logistics of travelling to Amritsar were far trickier than the family could have imagined. Train travel was unsafe, massacres of passengers from August to September of that year turned railway platforms and bogeys into charnel houses. Only in November were refugee specials arranged to transport people in relative safety. People went on foot, on camelback or in carts – whatever means they could find – and many were attacked en route. Buses groaned under the weight of desperate passengers. There was no question of carrying goods, people fled their homes with whatever little they could hide in their clothes or carry on their heads. The police had to be bribed with gold and money so that families could leave unmolested.

Historians describe it as the largest and bloodiest forced migration in recorded history, involving the displacement of 14 million people along religious lines. The authorities of the newly constituted nations were clearly not equipped to handle what would later be described as 'retributive genocide'. There is no accurate known marker of the death toll but estimates range from 200,000 to 2 million.

My mother vividly recalled the events of those days, as if they occurred just recently.

> The flag of Pakistan was flying around everywhere. My father owned a gun, and my brother Sudarshan and I were trained on how to use firearms. We knew we had to escape ... my father had saved very little money, since he was used to giving free medical treatment to many poor people. He took whatever money there was in the bank ... most of it went to the bus driver and conductor,

who were charging ₹ 300 for each ticket as buses around us were being attacked. We somehow managed to reach Lyallpur and stayed at a refugee camp.

The next trip was even trickier; the journey to Amritsar via train. But the train service to the east was erratic, and there was no guarantee that there wouldn't be a massacre on board. When the train service resumed, we left for the station in a military truck in the middle of the night.

We managed to board the train; another of my brothers, Suraj, got down to fetch water at a station, and got left behind, but luckily, found his way to Amritsar. At Amritsar, we stayed in the home of a Muslim who had vacated his house. In those days, we got *atta* (wheat flour) and even clothes as part of ration supplies.

The rest of the family also congregated at Amritsar and from there, we left for Panipat where my uncle worked in a factory that made blankets; he made arrangements for a room in the factory where we all stayed.

I gather from family lore that my grandparents had not wanted to move from Kamalia, until it was no longer a matter of choice. The town was in complete chaos and the situation was getting more dangerous by the hour. My grandparents couldn't bring themselves to believe there could be such an outpouring of hatred – 'that people were slaughtering one another'.

My father, who managed to escape along with the rest of the family, was in Delhi on the night of 14 August 1947. Like millions of his compatriots, he stayed up to hear Pandit Jawaharlal Nehru's historic 'Tryst with Destiny' speech on the radio. The following morning, he witnessed the first flypast by the Indian Air Force at Red Fort, in which a proud son of Lyallpur – Arjan Singh, then an acting Group Captain (later Chief of Air Staff and subsequently Marshal of the Indian Air Force), took part. He joined thousands of people who gathered at the Lahore Gate of Red Fort to witness Pandit Nehru raising the national flag for the first time on August 16, 1947.[7]

He experienced the bittersweet flavour of Independence and Partition to the fullest. On the one hand, he saw the celebrations on the streets, with people distributing sweets and flying the national flag outside their houses. On the other, he saw those same streets soaked in blood. He was staying in Paharganj, one of the worst-affected areas during the post-Partition riots.

Our family was among the lucky few who arrived in India unharmed, physically, at least. In those days, post-traumatic stress disorder or PTSD had not yet been identified and named, but many Partition refugees displayed its symptoms for years afterwards.

Uncle Satyanand was shattered. A man of peace who believed in the essential goodness of human nature, he was disturbed by the terrors he had seen and heard about. To add to it, his family had been uprooted and scattered. A harmonious, tightly knit and indomitable unit, the family was his whole world, and he was rebuilding the family home for all of them. Now, in the face of an uncertain future, his confidence that they could collectively weather any crisis had been undermined. Nevertheless he gradually began to pick up the pieces.

* *

Partition left India independent but in chaos. The province of Punjab was ripped in two, with inevitable economic and demographic consequences. Amritsar, called Ambarsar by its denizens, had become a border city. The Sikhs, who regarded Amritsar as the holiest seat of their faith, were relieved, even though they had been alienated from Nankana Sahib, regarded as the birthplace of Guru Nanak and Kartarpur Sahib, where he passed away (the Kartarpur corridor aims to allow visa-free access to this gurdwara now). Amritsar is the seat

7 As per the diary of Pamela Mountbatten, the daughter of Viceroy Louis Mountbatten, Nehru couldn't unfurl the Indian flag at Red Fort on August 15, 1947 because of the surging crowds; so he did it the next day.

of temporal power as well as the location of Shiromani Gurdwara Prabandhak Committee, which manages all the gurdwaras across the nation.

Amritsar was also a centre of tourism, attracting people from all over the world. They not only came to visit the Golden Temple and enjoy the city's famous cuisine, but also to visit the Durgiani Temple near the Lohgarh Gate. Built in 1921, in the architectural style of the Golden Temple, it was inaugurated by Pandit Madan Mohan Malaviya.

The city was a hub for trade and commerce. The biggest town in the region, it was the primary centre for trade in produce of the Himalayas, especially dry fruits, as well as exotic manufactured products from Samarkand, Persia, Afghanistan and Leh. The goods converged on Amritsar and were repacked and distributed all over the country. With no industry of its own, it was supported by Ludhiana, Jalandhar, Malerkotla and Phagwara. It was also the main education centre in the region, after Lahore.

Post-Partition, it was a place of turmoil since refugees had flooded in; border skirmishes were also frequent along with riots and agitations. The turbulent climate in Amritsar impacted the Munjals' fledgling business in bicycle parts and difficulties of those days remained forever etched in the minds of my uncles. I would sense a deep sadness in my uncle Om Prakash when he described that period. 'We had started from scratch … now we had to start all over again. We had to work very hard … we ran around … never bothered whether it was day or night … hammered crates … hammered nails … slept on floors, slept on platforms, sometimes in *dharamshala* (a building devoted to religious or charitable purpose, also serves as a rest house for travellers).' They were turbulent and testing times.

* *

My mother's family had settled in Panipat and it was here that my parents tied the nuptial knot in 1948. The *baraat* (wedding procession) embarked from Agra, where my father had joined his eldest brother, Bal

Mukund. All the brothers were on the move in search of opportunities, like thousands of other Partition refugees.

The family elders recall this period with great clarity. Uncle Sadanand had returned to Delhi and uncle Satyanand joined him. They were very close and wanted to stay together for as long as possible. In fact, popular in family lore is the tale of how his in-laws wanted uncle Satyanand and his family to move in with them when he reached Delhi, after the Partition. However, my uncle refused their offer, preferring to stay near his brother in a rented accommodation. At first, they lived in Pul Bangash, in Old Delhi. The two of them set up shop at the Red Fort cycle market off Esplanade Road in the vicinity of Chandni Chowk. The entire market would later be demolished by Sanjay Gandhi during the Emergency and another piece of our family history would be lost forever.

Meanwhile, uncle Bal Mukund had moved to Agra from Delhi and opened a bicycle business, and was joined by my father for a while. Their shop was located in the Cycle Mart, close to the Agra Red Fort which had been built by Akbar in 1573. Many small businesses proliferated in its shadow. My father later recalled, 'The Partition had unsettled everything and I was out of my own comfort zone, still struggling to find a future in the new emerging India.'

The income generated from the bicycle shop wasn't enough to sustain the Munjal family. My father also realized that remaining in Agra was futile, since it had very little to offer.

Fortuitously, my paternal grandfather's cousin, Satish Dhingra decided to set up a business in Delhi and invited my father to join him. He moved there, taking my mother with him. The couple lived in a small room provided by one of his friends.

My parents welcomed their first child into the world in 1949, whilst they had still been struggling to find their feet in Agra. It was a boy and they named him Raman Kant.

My father's joy was coloured by the pain of being unable to share his blessings with his family. His emotional ties to his siblings transcended physical separation and with Ramanji's arrival, he missed them all the more. He described that difficult period to me; how disoriented he felt, lying awake at night, staring at the ceiling and ruminating about his siblings, his parents and those halcyon times, in the not too distant past, when they had all lived under the same roof.

My mother was his emotional anchor. From her father, the civil surgeon at Samundri near Kamalia, she had inherited a fortitude that enabled her to hold the fort while my father travelled extensively. Like the Munjals, my mother's family were also followers of the *Arya Samaj*. Her parents held a *havan* every day and her father and mother were active philanthropists. She continued that tradition. With my father constantly on the move, trying out new ideas, my mother learnt to be self-sufficient.

The shop, 'Kalpurja' (machine parts) was located at Esplanade Road. The business dealt in bicycle tools, diesel engines and a variety of other spare parts for rail transport. It did well, thanks to my father's knack for anticipating the needs of the market. My father's job was to take orders from customers, source supplies and collect payments. On one occasion, my father went to Bombay to recover dues and managed to garner a set of fresh orders for Kalpurja. He spotted significant opportunities to grow the business out of Bombay and decided to settle down in the city, opening an engine parts shop, Laksmikant Bhandar.

* *

While my father was changing cities and exploring new vistas, his brothers Dayanand and Om Prakash had moved to Ludhiana. They did not realize it at the time, but my uncles could not have decided on a more appropriate base of operations.

It was an ancient town, with little infrastructure. Founded around a village called Mir Hota in the fifteenth century, it derives its name from the Lodhi dynasty (Lodhi-ana or town of the Lodhis). Remnants of its history can still be found on the outskirts of the town, where the ruins of the fort, built by Sikander Lodhi, still stand.

The town was briefly occupied by Maharaja Ranjit Singh in 1805, but he later ceded it to the British, who promptly established a permanent cantonment there. In 1947, a third of the population, comprising of Muslims, had decamped to Pakistan.

Centrally located, on the banks of the Sutlej and bang on the Grand Trunk Road, Ludhiana had immense potential. The void left by the Muslim community was quickly filled by enterprising refugees, the Munjals among them, who would power a quiet industrial revolution and turn it into the 'Manchester' of India. In later years, it would come to be known as the city of millionaires.

Uncle Dayanand, who was soon joined by uncle Om Prakash, set up a makeshift enterprise in bicycle spare parts and repairs on Gill Road. The idea was to provide them with employment and generate resources to keep the family afloat. Uncle Dayanand, foresaw a thriving market for bicycle parts, but could not have imagined that their small business would one day burgeon into a billion dollar empire. Of course, fate also played an important part in bringing the family together in a synergistic partnership that would alter the landscape of India.

* *

When my father decided to shift to Bombay to expand his business, Ramanji was just two years old. My mother would doubtless have preferred an apartment but initially, the family stayed at Hotel Trifle, which was located just behind the iconic Taj Mahal Hotel. My father often reminisced how South Bombay was like in the 1950s. The sea was a short walk from the hotel. The family would take a stroll to the Gateway of India or explore the Flora Fountain, a stone's throw from the Prince of Wales museum. They would watch the double-decker buses on Marine Drive and the trams winding their way from Bori Bunder to Dadar (the service was discontinued in 1964).

Bombay was the second commercial capital of India after Calcutta, home to the film industry and large businesses. My father was smitten by the eclectic mix of people, their professionalism and single-minded focus on achievement. Everyone, it appeared, was entrepreneurial and he found it exciting and exhilarating. My father's business in engine parts and machine tools, which he had set up in the city, began to prosper.

A great master of relationships, my father soon made friends among the Gujarati business community, who helped him nurture his business. He also became very close to a Sikh gentleman, Sardar Ishar Singh Chawla. He acquired fluency in English and cultivated a network of influential contacts, which helped the business grow. As the enterprise flourished, he also became skilled in handling the voluminous paperwork necessary in bidding for government contracts.

His became an important voice in the business community. Bringing people together was what he excelled at and he applied this talent to the world of business, helping fellow entrepreneurs find common ground and work with, rather than against each other. Many decades later, when he became the president of the Confederation of Engineering Industry (CEI) and a senior member of the Rotary movement, this experience would come in handy.

My father found like-minded souls among the dream merchants of Bombay, including film industry legends like O.P. Ralhan, Rajendra Kumar and I.S. Johar. He also got a taste of the high life. On some weekends, he would drive up to Lonavala or some other hill station with his family and friends, especially loving the Western Ghats during the monsoons. He developed a passion for automobiles and when his finances permitted, he acquired a Studebaker and, later, a Dodge.

Just when he had settled down in Bombay, nemesis dealt him a body blow. One of his main suppliers, who handled the procurement of machine parts and engines, abruptly disappeared with his money. My father was left with nothing.

Grief, hurt, humiliation and fear overwhelmed him and held him paralysed. He had taken an advance against the supply of machine parts and this meant that he would either have to renege on these contracts or pay back his clients. He was determined to make amends, not only because relationships were important to him but because he did not want to lose face. At all costs, he had to maintain his self-respect.

My father was in a dilemma about raising the money. He had put in an immense effort to build a life in Bombay. Success had brought a quiet satisfaction and a sense that things were finally under control, after a time of extreme uncertainty. By putting his faith in his main supplier, he fretted that he had once again toppled his family into an uneasy future.

My mother recalls that he would often spend his time pacing up and down his room, deeply troubled. Then one day, a telegram arrived. It was from uncle Dayanand. He wrote that their father was quite ill and it was imperative that my father go to Pul Bangash, in Old Delhi, where his parents were staying with uncle Sadanand and uncle Satyanand. The idea that he might lose his father threw mine into a panic. He left at once with his family, my mother recalls that they left everything behind; even the chulha (coal-fired stove) was left smouldering.

No sooner had he arrived, did he realize that the message had been a pretext to bring him and his family back to Pul Bangash in Old Delhi, within the protective fold of the family. He hadn't known it, but the family had heard of his run of bad luck in business through relatives and friends. The brothers felt it was time to rally around their sibling and extricate him from the mess. With great emotion my father would later recall: 'They did not want me to feel depressed or become mired in a sense of failure.'

At the age of thirty, he was ready to start again and rebuild what he had lost. First, he had to repay his debts, which would demand hard work. He had already taken legal recourse and filed cases against his erstwhile friend and supplier. The family, however, felt that he ought to let bygones be bygones and not waste time and money on lawyers and trips to Bombay. The loss of prestige was temporary, they told him and he would be better off putting his troubles behind him and joining the family business.

Soon after my father's arrival in Delhi, uncle Dayanand asked him to join the cycle business in Ludhiana. The growing market for bicycles and the mechanical skills of the local artisan community offered potential and uncle Dayanand felt that his younger brother was equipped with the skills to grow and develop the fledging business that he and uncle Om Prakash had started.

2

Laying the Foundations

Punjab Chief Minister Pratap Singh Kairon squinted through his spectacles, surveying the hubbub of activity that was the Hero Cycles factory. It was a beehive, packed with humming machines and workers in constant motion. A closer scrutiny nevertheless revealed a highly organized set of parallel activities being performed synchronously.

Bicycle kits were taking shape with a speed and efficiency that surprised and impressed Kairon. The CM was in the building, but not a single worker stopped to look at him. This dedicated workforce, he learnt, produced over a 31,000 bicycles a year. Kairon saw a company poised for growth and one that could genuinely bring investments and jobs to the state of Punjab. His faith in the promoters, the Munjal brothers, had been vindicated.

The Munjal brothers and their fledgling bicycle business had entered his radar screen soon after they set up the shed in Ludhiana. Whether it was Kairon who had broached the idea of bicycle manufacture with my father or the other way around, is not known but he certainly had a part to play in their migration from a shed to a proper factory.

The CM was intimately acquainted with the hunger to come good that characterized refugees from Pakistan Punjab, the Munjals among them. As state minister for rehabilitation, he had been in charge of resettling millions of migrants, a task he accomplished smoothly and rapidly, allotting them homes, land and job opportunities. He knew that sudden displacement and impoverishment had bred a deep sense of insecurity, a determination to regain what they had lost and an obsessive compulsion to carve a place for themselves in their new homeland. This became the driving force behind new enterprises, like Hero Cycles.

With the foresight that would earn him the accolade 'architect of modern Punjab', Kairon was keen on transforming Punjab from a purely agricultural state to an industrialized one and had focused on developing basic infrastructure like roads, power supply and irrigation. He implemented land reforms, set up educational institutions, played a key role in the establishment of Chandigarh and encouraged the growth of townships like Faridabad (which was a part of Punjab at that time).

He also mooted the establishment of the Punjab Agricultural University (PAU) on the pattern of US-style 'land grant colleges' (which he had learnt of while studying at the University of Michigan). The PAU was set up on 1,500 acres of land on the Ludhiana–Ferozepur highway. This institution would helm the Green Revolution, boosting agricultural productivity and ending India's humiliating dependence on food imports from the United States under the Public Law (PL) 480 regime. (Interestingly, many decades later, Hero Corporate Service set up an office in south Delhi, on the very site occupied by the US officials overseeing the PL 480 food-for-rupees programme in the 1960s!)

Behind all these efforts was the visionary CM's desire to put the state on the economic map of the country. For this, he needed the help of private entrepreneurs, like the Munjal brothers. Ludhiana was the leader in hosiery and woollens; why not bicycles? The Munjals were among the 128 small-scale units across India who had received licences to manufacture bicycles in 1956. The quota for this sector was limited to 2.5 lakh bicycles, however. The Munjals were not interested in a small-scale licence. As my father put it, 'We knew that with a small-scale licence, we would make money quickly, but something told us that if we somehow got into large-scale manufacturing, it could change the destiny of our family forever.'

The challenge was to convince the then Union Minister for Industry, Manubhai Shah, to tweak the 1956 Industrial Policy and remove the restriction on large-scale manufacturing of bicycles. That's where Kairon stepped in and convinced Manubhai Shah about the need to issue private entrepreneurs licenses to produce bicycles on a large scale. He was personally convinced that the Munjals and a few others like them had the wherewithal to deliver and, more importantly, the hunger to do so. As Kairon later told the brothers, 'I needed men with a fire in their bellies to grow and develop the state; and I saw this in you all.'

The Munjal brothers' decision to get into manufacturing was in keeping with the spirit of the times. In the early 1950s, India had embarked on a mixed economic growth model, based on five-year plans. Post-Independence, confronted by widespread poverty and a chronic lack of resources, policymakers felt rapid industrialization was the way forward. The first Five-Year Plan launched in 1951 emphasized the role of the public sector but also sought to support the growing private sector.

Transportation was an acute requirement, as the growth in freight and passenger traffic in the preceding years had put tremendous strain on the Indian Railways and the public was requested to 'travel only when you must'. Manifestly, there was a vast market for personal transportation.

When my father, the ideas man, had first proposed the idea of manufacturing to his siblings back in the early 1950s, they had expressed their reservations. In those days, bicycle parts and components were by and large imported. The supplies were tightly controlled by a cartel, comprising of the old British agency houses, which had been passed on to Indian associates post-Independence. These entities doled out supplies on a quota basis. My uncle Om Prakash remembered having to wait for two whole days at the offices of Dunlop (suppliers of tyres and tubes), just to meet the manager.

* *

My father was persuasive and was confident that they had the know-how to manufacture bicycles, but that dream would be stillborn if India's dependence on imported parts and components continued. He proposed that the brothers manufacture their own but they protested, pointing out that technology and capital were both scarce. Even before the *karigars* (artisans) could get down to making components, tools and dyes would have to be created. Everything would have to be done from scratch, on a shoestring budget.

In subsequent chapters, I will describe how these supply and capital constraints impelled the Munjal brothers to create a supply chain that would become the cynosure of the manufacturing world. For the moment, let me describe the Indian bicycle industry of the era, which was growing in fits and starts.

The first complete bicycle had been manufactured in India in 1938, by the India Cycle Manufacturing Company in Calcutta. It was quickly followed by Hind Cycles in Bombay and Hindustan Bicycles in Patna. All through the 1940s though, the majority of demand was met via imports, because Indian-made bicycles were of poorer quality, clumsy and with an average life of only a few years. The fledgling industry was granted protection from foreign competition in the mid-1950s, resulting in a number of new units coming up, including Atlas Cycles in Sonepat. Hind Cycles quickly became a market leader, accounting for the bulk of Indian-made bicycles.

For the Munjal brothers, Ludhiana offered a locational advantage. It had already become a hub for light engineering, with motor works, small machine tools and pump manufacturing units dotting the cityscape. Ludhiana's population, a mere 8,75,000 in 1951, was growing rapidly and only Amritsar and Jalandhar were more populous.

The atmosphere in Ludhiana of the 1950s and 1960s is best described by business historian Gita Piramal, in her book, *Business Maharajas* (Penguin India):

> Picture for yourself, India at that moment in time, a country racked by famines and droughts, its industrial machinery devastated by the demands made on it by World War II, no friends in the world, no foreign exchange, no reserves. So, naturally, Nehru and the administration of the time invited entrepreneurs to build the new temples, which would create wealth for the country.
>
> Many entrepreneurs took the opportunity; amongst them were bicycle makers, bicycles were in big demand at that time ... groups like the Birlas with Hind Cycles, TI in the south, they all jumped on to this bandwagon. The Munjals were one of them, in fact, they knew the business better than most and their centre of operation would be Ludhiana.

A brief digression is necessary here. While my uncles Dayanand and Om Prakash were packing up to move to Ludhiana, one of their suppliers, a Muslim by the name of Kareem Deen, was preparing to shift to Pakistan. He manufactured bicycle saddles under a brand name he had created himself. Before he left, Kareem Deen went to see his friend Om Prakash Munjal.

What happened next would be a life-changing moment for our family. Uncle Om Prakash asked Kareem Deen whether the Munjals could use that brand name for their business. He agreed. The gesture was typical of the way businesses were run at the time – on reputation, relationships and goodwill. The worth and value of brands and patents were not appreciated or understood. And so, with nothing more than a casual nod, his brand passed to the Munjals.

Yes, dear reader, you guessed correctly. It was 'Hero'.

* *

Once my uncles came around to the idea of manufacturing, a confident, '*Yeh bhi kar lenge*' (We can do this too), resounded around the Munjal residence and workplace. Walking the talk was another kettle of fish, of course.

At the time, there were no manufacturing manuals laying out engineering designs and production processes. The Munjals had to wing it and create their own heuristics. My father and uncle Om Prakash would squat in the backyard with the artisans, drawing designs of cycle parts on sheets of paper and discussing ways of implementing them. The end product was assembled by hand and then put through multiple functionality tests. Unknowingly, this bottom-up approach created an advantage of quality and consistency.

Their very first experiment in 1954, was in bicycle forks (which they had been supplying to Atlas), the part that holds the wheel. A small furnace was set up in the backyard of the shop, with two workers and a foreman to oversee the manufacturing process. After several hits and misses, they finally came up with a product that satisfied all the siblings.

Yet disaster soon struck and almost cost the Munjals their business. The welding in some of the bicycle forks cracked and the pipes broke off with the result that the incensed dealers returned all orders. The siblings pooled their resources and paid back the affected parties, no questions asked. Their reputation survived, but their pockets were almost empty.

The Munjal brothers girded their loins, went back to the design table and perfected the forks. As none of their dealers had suffered any losses, they were willing to take a chance on the forks again and this time round, there were no glitches. The Munjal business had survived by the skin of its teeth.

Satisfied with the fork, my father turned his attention to bicycle handles, which were even harder to come by. S.K. Rai (who was to join the business in 1983 and become a de facto member of the family), recalls hearing descriptions of just how challenging the scenario was at the time. He spent a lot of time with my father, who would recount stories of those early days of struggle: 'After some time, the supplier of bicycle handles started asking for exorbitant prices. He knew, of course, that he enjoyed a monopoly and without his product, there was no bicycle'. My father did not want to be at his mercy!

The Munjal brothers turned to the local community of *mistris* (technicians), artisans and craftsmen, the Ramgarhias, to untangle their knotty technical problems. Members of the Ramgarhia community weren't really technically qualified in the formal sense, but were held in high esteem by the entire clan and the workmen. My father, in particular, enjoyed an excellent understanding with these worthies.

He once tried to explain the importance of the Ramgarhia *mistris* in the Munjal scheme of things: 'They are born artisans, and their skills are passed on from generation to generation.[8] They had already started manufacturing certain bicycle parts and when people like us, who could bring them the samples and offer a market, came along – well, it created a perfect synergy, levering their ability to make parts, and our commercial strength.'

When he asked the Ramgarhias and other skilled artisans to try their hand at making handlebars from scratch, the master craftsmen allowed themselves to be persuaded, due to ties of affection and a respect for

---

[8] Two of India's finest cricketers, spinner Harbhajan Singh and fast bowler Jasprit Bumrah – who are considered masters of their craft – also belong to the Ramgarhia community.

my father's judgement. After the initial hiccups, the experiment was an outstanding success. The handlebars were Munjal-worthy and only the plating had to be outsourced.

Members of the Ramgarhia community left an imprint and had an impact on the Hero ecosystem for several years. In the 1960s, Atma Singh played an important role in tool design at Rockman Industries, one of the first family run ancillary units that my father and uncles set up. Atma Singh wasn't technically qualified, but was an absolute master at his craft, so much so that he could replicate machine tools by simply looking at photographs. Swaran Singh, and Ramgarhia Bansal were other members of the Ramgarhia community responsible for the successful emergence of the indigenous supply chain of Hero Cycles in the early decades along with Amrik Singh, who came from Hindustan Machine Tools (the public sector firm which made the famous HMT watches and tractors in the 1970s to the 1990s).

Back to the story on bicycle parts. The handlebars were made in Ludhiana; the mudguard came from Bahadurgarh. In the 1950s, uncle Satyanand set up a factory along with my other uncle Sadanand to manufacture these bicycle parts at Bahadurgarh, encouraged by the government to populate this less developed part of Punjab.[9]

After the mudguard came the question of the frame.

My father insisted that the bicycle be designed keeping Indian conditions in mind. It had to be capable of carrying more than two people, plus a heavy load, retail at the lowest possible price, and be seen as the people's mode of transport. He spoke from firsthand experience – in those early years, all three brothers piled on to a single bicycle to get from their home in Model Town to the shop on Gill Road!

The Hero cycle had to be a workhorse. The milkman should be able to affix his cans to the carrier, and the farmer his basket of vegetables. Durability was another priority. My father wanted a bicycle that could

9 Bahadurgarh is part of the state of Haryana today. Punjab was split into two states as part of the Punjab Reorganisation Act in 1966.

literally be handed down from one generation to the next. Maintenance and repairs had to be simple and spare parts easily available.

Finally, the brothers were ready to assemble the first 100 per cent Hero-made bicycle. From tip to tail, it would be their baby, except for the rim which was from a company known as Regent, while the tyres and tubes were purchased from Dunlop. My father and uncles were in a fever of excitement as the artisans went to work.

A few hours later, there she stood: a vision in chrome and black, her glossy curves an invitation to intrepid travellers: the very first Hero bicycle.

My father couldn't wait to try it out, riding it around the cramped space of the workshop's backyard. The smooth action of the pedals, the feel of the wheels skimming the ground, responding to the slightest turn of the handlebars, was to stay with him forever. His first thought was to share the joy of that moment with his family. Off he went, pedalling home to his loved ones, over dirt tracks and insufferable roads, by the light of a rising moon.

'Brijmohanji would share that golden moment with me; of riding this bicycle to his home late in the evening around 8 p.m. and excitedly presenting it to his family,' recalls Mr Rai.

My father kept that bicycle for a long time. It was his prized possession and in many ways a metaphor for my father's life. He said: 'I have always seen myself as a traveller and an adventurer. My journey has been similar to riding/driving down a road towards a fixed destination. If I came across roadblocks or speed-breakers, I would slow down. If there were rough patches, I shifted to different gears, never stopping nor losing faith.'

Events moved swiftly thereafter. In 1956, Hero Cycles was registered with a seed capital of ₹50,000 and got its manufacturing licence. The company commenced operations with a first-year production of 639 bicycles, this grew rapidly to 7,803 bicycles in the following year and then, to 31,000 bicycles a year by 1961.

After manufacturing, the next big challenge was distribution. Fortunately, uncle Om Prakash had some solid experience and domain expertise in this area. Prior to making bicycles on a large scale, the brothers were making and selling a few bicycle parts from their Ludhiana shed; uncle Om Prakash was given the responsibility of sales. He had spent a number of years in the field, developing a distribution network, undertaking extensive tours of states like Uttar Pradesh and Rajasthan. At first, he found it difficult to convince dealers who were sceptical about the capabilities of a company situated in faraway Punjab, and the days went by without a single order. Family elders say uncle Dayanand was so incensed that he shot off a telegram to his younger brother: 'You seem to be useless in this business, you should come back.'

Uncle Om Prakash recounted how upset he was at his elder brother's admonition but it galvanized him and made him more determined to prove himself. He approached Baldev, the proprietor of a shop in Kanpur, who had previously shown no interest in his wares. No sooner did Baldev see him than he roared: 'Why have you come back again? I am not interested in your product!'

'You will like the product when you see it, sir,' my uncle told him. He opened his bag and laid out the gleaming range of bicycle components on the proprietor's desk. After subjecting them to close examination, Baldev realized they were of exceptional quality. He placed a generous order. When the delivery arrived, Baldev was stunned; a member of his staff told him that the order did not tally. He calmed down when he was told that instead of a hundred bicycle kits, there were 104, but the billing was only for the order that had been placed. When Baldev called my uncle to point out the error to him, the latter told him that the excess had been intentional. Baldev would go on to become one of Hero Cycle's longest-standing dealers, with a relationship that would span over half a century.

When the success was reported to uncle Dayanand, he shot off another telegram: 'Keep it up!'

* *

City by city, day by day, uncle Om Prakash built a wide network of distributors for bicycle components, through sheer perseverance and relentless dedication. He travelled third class by rail, stayed only in the cheapest hotels and worked all through the day. And like my father, he invested in relationships, even at the cost of profit.

The family discovered the difficult conditions in which uncle Om Prakash operated to build his famed dealers' network only when my father accompanied him on a sales trip for the first time. He was mortified when they boarded the third-class compartment of a train to Nagpur. My father asked him if this was how he always travelled, to which his brother replied in the affirmative.

A further shock awaited my father when they landed in the city and checked into the hotel where my uncle usually stayed. The accommodation was appalling and he asked his brother why he stayed in such dubious lodgings, when the company could afford better?

My uncle shot back: 'It's clean, its vegetarian, it's close to the market and it's only three rupees a night.'

My father held his peace, but when they returned to Ludhiana, he headed straight to their manager and instructed him to ensure that his brother travelled by first class, took taxis to meet dealers and stayed in decent, well-appointed hotels! In many ways, this reflected the different style and approach of the two brothers towards business and life. Uncle Om Prakash was always looking for ways to get the job done at the least possible cost; my father just wanted to get it done right!

In the span of a year, uncle Om Prakash established more than 500 dealerships across India. His efforts would give Hero Cycles an edge over their existing competitors, such as Raleigh and Atlas Cycles.

During this period, established players like Hercules and Atlas enjoyed considerable goodwill and a large market share. My father, as always, was not deterred by competitors. Hansraj Pahwa of Avon Cycles, and the Kapoors of Atlas Cycles were among Hero's biggest competitors, yet became some of my father's closest friends. The Murugappa family, which owned TI Cycles, were also friends. Hero eventually pedalled its way past all of them, but I never detected the slightest hint of triumphalism in my father or my uncles.

Later, when Hero entered the automotive market, he was just as gracious in his dealings with Rahul Bajaj of Bajaj Auto, who wrote that he had fondly regarded my father as his guru.

'Over the years, we fought very fiercely in the marketplace, first with Hero Honda and, then, with Hero MotoCorp. There was no give and take. Yet, we remained very good friends all these years. Whenever we met, he gave me tremendous regard and I received genuine love and affection, which was not the case with some of my other competitiors,' he observed in an article. Over a forty-year relationship, Rahul Bajaj said, he hadn't heard a single negative thing about my father.

'Hard is trying to rebuild yourself, piece by piece, with no instruction book, and no clue as to where all the important bits are supposed to go,' says Nick Hornby, in *A Long Way Down*. That's how it was for the Munjals as they set about building the Hero brand.

Each brother played a role. If uncle Dayanand was the one who held the family together and held the fort at the production end, uncle Satyanand took responsibility for quality, uncle Om Prakash was the sales and distribution genius and my father was the visionary. He did not look for markets, he created them by always being up to date on the latest technology and looking for new ways to develop the business. Every time he came across a new part or component, he would try and figure out how it could be incorporated by Hero.

By the late 1950s, the company was poised for expansion, and once again, my father took the lead. What was the point of having a large-scale licence if you couldn't acquire scale? All at once, it occurred to him that he wouldn't find the answers in Ludhiana. It was time to expand his horizons. That's how he wound up on an airplane, for the first time in his life.

* *

At Düsseldorf airport one crisp September morning in 1959, a middle-aged man paced up and down, awaiting the arrival of the Air India flight from Delhi. His name was Ernest Mann and he was a business consultant. He was to receive a businessman from India, by the name of Brijmohan Lall Munjal. He knew Mr Munjal only as a voice on the phone, speaking English in an Indian accent.

My father had got in touch with him through a network of acquaintances involved in the import of bicycle components from Europe. Mann scanned the airport as he paced, looking for someone in Indian attire. After a while, he made his way to the airport enquiry desk, where he spotted a wheat-complexioned individual in a natty black three-piece suit. Perhaps this gentleman could help.

'I am expecting a guest from India, someone involved in bicycle engineering. Have you seen anyone in Indian attire ... you know, that cloth around the lower body and the mark on the forehead?' he asked.

My father replied, 'I am from India and I am from Hero Cycles. Are you Mr Mann?'

The German trader stared at him for a moment, then apologized for his faux pas and hugged him by way of welcome.

Fresh out of Ludhiana, my father was clad in the businessman's uniform, his hair slicked down with a liberal application of Brylcream and crowned with a hat. He had landed at Düsseldorf after a long, hopping flight on an Air India propeller aircraft (the first jet, a Boeing 707, was introduced the following year).

When he had broached the idea of looking for business connections abroad, his brothers were reluctant to let him go. The Air India crash of 1950 lingered in public memory. They gave in eventually, but were apprehensive even as he entered the airport. '*Kahan jayega*? *Kaise hoga*?' (Where will you go? How will you manage?)'

No one from the family had travelled on an airplane, much less taken an international flight yet my father was determined. A large part of the family showed up to see him off at the airport in Delhi. Taking a flight, particularly an international one, was a very big deal in those days. There was much excitement, especially among the children, at the prospect of actually seeing an airplane close-up.

In Düsseldorf, my father was on a mission and he believed that the German was just the 'Mann' who would help him achieve it. A light blue Mercedes rolled up, the two hopped in and soon were on the road. That was when my father fell in love with the European countryside. Fond of long drives, he was spellbound by the pristine scenery, interspersed with modern buildings and traditional cottages, unlike anything he had ever seen. What excited him even more were the conversations with Mann, which revolved around engineering.

My father's purpose was to acquire cutting-edge technology of the era for Hero, so Mann and he held a long discussion on the manufacture of bicycle chains and debated the merits of rival manufacturers. They visited two factories that made bicycle chain machines, one at Wuppertal and the other at Heimer in the North Rhine Westphalia region east of Düsseldorf. The engineers at the facilities were impressed by the Indian businessman's encyclopaedic knowledge of bicycle components. Here was a businessman accustomed not only with merchandising and shop floor operations but the technical specifications of his machines. Eventually, my father placed his order with Mann, whose facility was located at Heimer.

At this point, Hero Cycles was still a small company, but that didn't stop my father from visualizing on a grander canvas. This entrepreneurial spirit appealed to the Germans. By the time his tour ended, he was armed with fresh technical knowledge and a plethora of contacts. He also understood, for the first time, how technology could be used to gain an edge over competition.

My father returned home in triumph, having established a firm friendship with Mann, who would prove to be a valuable contact and more important, a mentor. Two German-made bicycle chain manufacturing plants had been purchased, at a cost which made his siblings gasp, but would give Hero a long-lasting edge over the competition. Throughout his life, he would always acknowledge Mann's contribution to the success of Hero.

'Mann showed me the importance of technology; how technology helped improve and standardize production; he also showed me how to negotiate and get the best technology at the best possible price,' my father told me.

The trip was memorable for reasons other than business. At the age of thirty-six, my father saw the monorail for the first time. He captured it on film, having had the foresight to carry a camera. He wanted to document his travels, so that he could share them with his family. In any case, he loved gizmos and thoroughly enjoyed trying out his camera.

My father's tour of Germany was the first of many. He got to know the country so well, that Mr Rai, who accompanied him on a tour a couple of decades later, said, 'He seemed to know Germany like the back of his hand ... he knew every turning in the roads we took.'

My father buzzed around the globe to source world-class components and machines. He recalled those years: 'I went first to Germany for some years and then to Japan and I started bringing in the modern equipment for manufacturing bicycle components. I think I can claim that I took bicycle-making to a different level than was being done then. Germany, at that time, was really dominant in the machine and tools business and I bought a complete chain-making plant for ₹300,000.'

By the early 1960s, when Chief Minister Kairon visited the factory, Hero Cycles was a thriving enterprise. The Munjal family naturally had a deep regard for the iconic statesman and his assassination in 1965 came as a huge blow; the only consolation was that he did not live to see the trifurcation of the state through the Punjab Reorganization Act of 1966, against which he had fought throughout his political career.

3

A Family That Works Together, Stays Together

Strong family ties enabled the Munjals to power through many of the challenges that came in the way of building the Hero brand: the crooked dealers and suppliers looking to make a quick buck, petty officials who indulged in gratuitous harassment, a maze of bureaucratic paperwork at every step and competitors undermining the fast-growing company; there were an endless list of hurdles.

Bahadur Chand Munjal, my grandfather, passed away in 1960 after ailing for several years and uncle Dayanand took on the role of family patriarch. Injury et al, he was still a force to reckon with in the family. He was the go-to person for all issues whether business or personal, and often cheered his younger siblings on, encouraging and prodding them to excel. At the worst of times, he displayed an amazing resilience, getting the family to look at the lighter side of life. For my father and uncle, his word was law and his writ extended across the entire family.

It was uncle Dayanand who had discovered his younger brother Om Prakash's talent for poetic composition. Having heard one of his poems, uncle Dayanand challenged him to write another, on his newborn son. Uncle Om Prakash composed a couplet on the spot. His older brother was overwhelmed, and urged his younger sibling never to give up on his poetry. He never did.

My uncle remained passionate about poetry all his life and could conjure the most appropriate impromptu couplets at the drop of a hat. He was known as the poetic Munjal and was credited with putting Ludhiana on the cultural map of India. He was famous for his *shayari* in the Urdu literary circuit. The *mushairas* (an evening social gathering at which Urdu poetry is read, typically taking the form of a contest) and other cultural events that he organized were also legendary in the world of artistes.

Noted Urdu poet Kewal Dheer, in fact, once credited my uncle with keeping Urdu poetry alive in north India. Their's was an association that almost spanned half a century – forty-six years to be exact. Dheer, who was extremely fond of uncle Om Prakash, said: 'People knew him for his industrial acumen, but he was equally popular in literary circles for his love for Urdu poetry. He remembered many couplets and recited them to suit the occasion. He was the chief patron of Adeeb International Society, which organized Jashn-e-Sahir and many other activities throughout the year.'

Uncle Om Prakash's education had come to a premature halt when he joined the cycle shop in Amritsar at the age of sixteen. Although he would always maintain that he did not regret his interrupted education, perhaps it did rankle, because he was naturally blessed with a great hunger for knowledge. In later decades, he encouraged us, the next generation of Munjals, to get a good education. Yet whenever we questioned him in this regard, he would brush our queries aside, saying, 'Life is the biggest teacher and the world is the biggest school. When I make a mistake, I learn and grow bigger. Although I never went to college, I never failed to learn.'

Like my father, uncle Om Prakash was a great orator, who could hold an audience transfixed. He was known for greeting visitors with an appropriate *sher*. After a couple of meetings, his acquaintances would begin to look forward to his couplets and anticipate which one he would recite. My father was fond of music too, but he preferred a different oeuvre. Among his favourites were ghazal singer Jagjit Singh and the doyens of the 1950s, like Suraiya and K.L. Saigal.

Uncle Om Prakash was the creative spirit behind the Hero Diary, which became something of a collector's item. Every page had a proverb, or a couplet carefully selected by him from among the works of poets across the country. He would spend hours every day, poring over the proofs in an effort to get each page exactly right. Many of the couplets were original, as poets would vie with each other to find a place in the Hero Diary. The print run in the late 1960s ran into tens of thousands and still fell short of demand. Several people I know collected the diaries over the years.

Back to the family patriarch. Uncle Dayanand intrinsically believed that there was more to business than the profit motive and more to life than just business. Family came first and by family, he meant the clan, their friends, business associates and employees. He was a people person, unfailingly warm and loving and few could have guessed that he was in constant pain from the injury he sustained during the Quetta earthquake.

He also ensured that the brothers lived close together. Initially, when uncle Satyanand came to Ludhiana with his family, he lived in a rented house along with his family. The proprietor later offered the house to him for outright purchase, but his elder brother felt it was too far away and insisted that Satyanand find a house close to the rest of the brothers. This was in Ludhiana's Model Town which was set up to accommodate refugees from Pakistan. The Munjal homes adjoined each other, forming a colony within a colony!

Whatever money they earned, the brothers put back into the bicycle business, thus there was barely anything left over to purchase homes. So the family members moved in initially as tenants. Uncle Dayanand was in number 21, uncle Om Prakash and my father occupied the right and left wings of number 26, uncle Satyanand was in number 24, my aunt Santosh was in 232, uncle Sadanand was in 231, uncle Bal Mukund in 39 and so on. The Munjals eventually purchased these homes and continued to live here, for as long as the family remained in the city.

Uncle Dayanand and uncle Om Prakash set a tradition of family get-togethers, at festivals or celebrations of anniversaries and weddings. Regardless of where they happened to be at that point in time, it was incumbent on all members to attend. Over elaborate meals, our grandmother and uncle Om Prakash regaled youngsters with stories and anecdotes that, unbeknownst to them, instilled moral values and a sense of history. I remember hearing tales of the Partition and what life had been like then, and marvelling at my family's never-say-die resilience and joie de vivre.

When I look back, there are these amazing memories of large gatherings with family and friends, I recall the festive spirit in which they were held. Indeed, many of these get-togethers would take place around festivals or events that took place in the family. My favourite time of the year was *Baisakhi* (a harvest festival in the state of Punjab) when the entire family would pile into buses and cars and head to Doraha, on the outskirts of Ludhiana. It was a riverside town of perhaps 30,000 people and we would sit by the river and have a picnic, revelling in the warm feeling of togetherness.

Uncle Om Prakash would continue the tradition even after uncle Dayanand passed away, creating occasions for family congregations while constantly fostering a spirit of affectionate closeness.

⁂ ⁂

If my father and uncles were the support structure on which the family business rested, their wives were the fretwork, as they presided over a vast, amalgamated household. Uncle Om Prakash had married my aunt Sudarshan in 1953 and they now had a large family of their own, comprising of four daughters and a son.

Aware that uncle Om Prakash needed to travel extensively to build the dealership network, she knew that being away from the family could take a toll on his spirit. To encourage aunt Sudarshan to accompany him on his long tours, my mother often took charge of their children.

At any given time my mother had ten children to look after. Our families mirrored each other; my parents had four sons and a daughter and my uncle and aunt had four daughters and a son. My mother managed us all with aplomb. My father and uncle had purchased interconnected houses, with a courtyard and common verandah for the children to play in and separate kitchens, which were available to all of us. 'There wasn't much money, but those were good times,' my mother recalled.

Like most children growing up, we fought and argued amongst ourselves as often as we played and bonded. The fact that our natures were different, often led to interesting outcomes.

I remember the time when my father owned just a single small car, so whenever my parents went out there was space to accommodate just one child at the back. Most of us kids fought and jostled one another to get in. When we reached the car, Pawan would already be seated. He anticipated the skirmish, and made his moves in advance! This happened not once, but on several occasions.

'Chachaji' Om Prakash was very strict, so the Munjal children – myself included – tended to tread lightly around him. He was as loving as he was tough, so we didn't take his occasional scoldings to heart. One my early memories of him is the little pad he kept on his bedside table and attached to it was a pencil on a string. He would scribble in it every now and then. In the morning, before he left for work, he would tear off the page of notes and take it with him. There was also a little book on life lessons that he would read every morning, without fail.

He read a great deal, mainly non-fiction. An Urdu newspaper was delivered to the house and both he and my father would take turns to read it. In later years, if I found a book or an article of interest, I kept it aside for my uncle to browse through and he would remember what he had read and use it when the occasion demanded.

There were also the famous washbasins, the stuff of family legend, located on either side of the courtyard (we lived on the left side of the said *aangan* and my uncle's family on the right). There was a general agreement within the family that these innocuous ceramic bowls had played a pivotal role in building the Hero empire.

I don't know how they timed it, but each morning, my father and uncle found a way to appear at their respective washbasins at exactly the same moment, armed with their shaving kits. Business matters would be discussed as they lathered up and scraped away; ideas were shared, notes exchanged and crucial decisions taken. It was a morning ritual with them for as long as I can remember and they religiously stuck to it until my father moved to Delhi.

They had very different personalities. My father was a restless soul, always on the go, looking for new frontiers in business and technology. My uncle was perfectly content staying back in Ludhiana to manage operations (except in the early days, when he was setting up the dealer network). Unlike my father, he was short-tempered.

Every employee at Hero Cycles knew that if O.P. Munjal gave you a job to do, you had to accomplish it within the given time frame, or be prepared for an explosion. He would follow up relentlessly, refusing to accept excuses that were non-existent. Ruthlessly efficient himself, he had no time for negligence or incompetence. Nor did he suffer fools gladly, or at all. He was also a tough negotiator and no one could slip anything by him.

My father, by contrast, was gentler by nature. He had an expansive personality and went to great lengths to put people at ease. He was the ideas man, while his brother was the execution ninja. They melded their respective talents into a highly progressive and efficient enterprise.

* *

No matter how busy our parents were, they always had time for us, for me, in particular. I had been born with a club foot, which meant that I spent the first thirteen years of my life in and out of hospitals. My father would show up at the hospital every morning with milk, tea and snacks and make friends with all the doctors. My early travails created a special bond with my parents. Till she passed away, I was the only one my mother turned to when she was feeling unwell (as my father did for several years), and unless I accompanied her, she kept putting off a visit to the doctor, for any kind of ailment.

My mother handled her large, bustling household with a light touch. She never complained or appeared overwhelmed and held the fort while my father travelled, which was often. He never came home empty-handed. Typical of his nature, there would be gifts for everyone and those for his sons would be as alike as possible. A family picture from the early 1960s shows all four of us in identical leather shorts. The joyful moment of my father walking in through the door, hugging us all and then, like a magician producing a rabbit from his hat, delving into his baggage and placing a gift in our hands, was repeated many times during our childhood. I must confess to having received a larger share of toys, which I preserved and ceremoniously handed over to my nephew, Rahul, when he was born.

In 1957, the year I was born, my father bought a car – his first since those awful reverses in Bombay. Perhaps business had picked up by that time. Or perhaps he was just tired of cycling to the office every day, taking a shortcut over the fields because there were no proper roads.

* *

When my cousin Yogesh, uncle Satyanand's eldest son the eldest among us, graduated from Roorkee University (later upgraded to an Indian Institute of Technology or IIT) with a degree in engineering, he was asked to join uncle Dayanand at Rockman Cycles, the first of many ancillary units, which was set up in 1960. Thus began another Munjal tradition, of youngsters from the next generation interning with their uncles or older cousins when they joined the family business. More on this later.

It was a rigorous internship, but Yogesh still has enduring memories of our uncle's large-heartedness. Yogesh says, 'I joined in January, 1964. I was in Hero Cycles for a few months and then placed with uncle Dayanand because he was not keeping well.'

My mother always said that uncle Dayanand had a great ability to adjust. 'He used to greet everyone with warmth and love. He lived separately from his mother, but made sure that he spent every evening with her, when he returned from work. He was gregarious and had the best interest of everyone at heart which was why the family loved and respected him a great deal.'

In the evening, all the brothers would meet, sit around my grandmother and take turns to press her feet. Her grandchildren, myself included, would also take turns to perform this little service and receive her blessings each time we did. She would recite verses from the *Guru Granth Sahib* and we would repeat them with her. Yogesh recalls that before she passed away, she left instructions that her *Guru Granth Sahib bir* (copy) be taken to the gurdwara, 'since all of you are *Arya Samaj*is'. As was the custom, Yogesh said: 'We put the *Guru Granth Sahib* on our heads and carried it to the gurdwara.'

Naturally, when the question of Yogesh's marriage came up, uncle Satyanand referred the proposal to his elder brother. It was he who discussed the matter with the prospective bride's father and took a final call. Yogesh reminisces about uncle Dayanand's role in fixing his marriage: 'He called me to Rockman to meet the family, asked me to see the girl and finalize the match.'

As the family fortunes picked up, so did the education levels amongst the next generation of Munjals. Uncle Om Prakash, ever conscious of his own interrupted education, sent his children to Sanawar. My older siblings had gone to local schools in Ludhiana – Ramanji to Arya Mandir and Pawan and Suman to St Joseph's Academy and thereafter, to Punjab Public School in Nabha. Originally a military school, it had made a name for itself in academics. After a year at the Sacred Heart Convent in Ludhiana in Class III, I followed my brothers to Nabha.

A couple of years later, I sat for and cleared the common entrance exam and opted for the Doon School. However, there was a small twist.

My headmaster at Nabha was a buddy of my father's (his network of friends was truly astonishing), and told him that he would not allow me to leave. I was in a fix. Eventually, thanks to my cousin Suraksha's persuasive skills, I went off to Dehradun. At the time, Ramanji was in Manipal studying engineering (he later shifted to Patiala). I was more interested in medicine, but somehow, ended up studying engineering like my siblings – all the better to add value to the Hero Group!

As the Munjal family evolved and its progeny grew up, they were given the opportunity to capture real-time experiences and apply their intellect and skills to the business. It wasn't always a smooth ride, especially as the years passed, and the family's affluence grew.

I remember within the family, a role assigned to me by my father was to help the members of the third generation, the youngsters. One of the difficulties I faced was to make sure that talent matched the appropriate role, so there was quite a bit of rigour involved. This meant that before final placement, the youngsters coming into the business were put through tough situations. There is no exact science to the level of difficulties that the youngsters encountered and some had a tougher time than the others. However, uniformly and across the board, the impact of the grind was visible in their performance and achievements in later years.

One of the complications and difficulties of this approach was the perception amongst the parents of their children's capabilities, especially the mothers. I remember when one of the ladies in the family told me that her son was probably one of the smartest in the family, and we had unnecessarily given him in a tough (but basic) role. She had expected his being allotted a significant responsibility straight away, on joining the family business. It was hard to explain to her, that not only was the young man not the smartest, but he also had a lot to learn before reaching his full potential!

* *

In 1961, uncle Satyanand also moved to Ludhiana. As mentioned earlier, my uncles Sadanand and Satyanand had set up a factory in Bahadurgarh, on the outskirts of Delhi where mudguards and power presses were manufactured. Initially, it made very little progress. Uncles Satyanand and Sadanand were constantly irked by the absence of a work ethic and handicapped by the fact that there was no readymade market for their products. Nor was there an ecosystem for manufacturing since Bahadurgarh in those days didn't have a single hardware store or grinding mill.

My cousin Yogesh used to tell us, 'Even to buy one screw or a nail, my father had to send a person to Delhi by bus to get supplies from Chawri Bazaar; as a result it became very difficult to repair machines on time.' A *mistri* from the Hero Cycles tool room in Ludhiana was sent to Bahadurgarh to assist uncles Satyanand and Sadanand. He lived in the factory premises and applied his mechanical skills to the operations. Soon, the factory was producing mudguards of adequate standard, but business never really picked up for reasons that were beyond the control of my two uncles.

What made matters worse was that during the monsoon, water from a nearby nullah overflowed and flooded the factory premises. Uncle Satyanand, thoroughly fed up, closed the factory and decided to permanently relocate to Ludhiana and join his brothers at Hero Cycles.

Even though the factory was shut down, there were a few unintended but positive outcomes, Yogesh recalls. 'The mistri later struck out on his own. He established a plant along the same lines as the one in Bahadurgarh and went on to become a successful entrepreneur.'

Uncle Satyanand's siblings were delighted to have him in Ludhiana (while uncle Satyanand shifted to Ludhiana, uncle Sadanand decided to stay back in Delhi). Hero Cycles was growing and his practical experience and wisdom were a blessing, at a time when his siblings, Brijmohan and Om Prakash, were travelling frequently, the former to source new technology and the latter to build and grow the dealership network. He took over the day-to-day management of the factory along with uncle Dayanand and maintained its quality standards impeccably. Shoddy work was not permitted on his watch.

Eventually, uncle Bal Mukund also came to Ludhiana. The bicycle shop he and my father had managed in Agra had languished. Thereafter, he explored the possibility of entering the leather business, but nothing came of it. He eventually decided to try his hand at trading in coal. He had spent a few years in Sindh in the 1930s working in the coal sector and was familiar with it, plus, coal was in great demand, not only for the Indian Railways but to power burgeoning new industries.

After four years in the coal business in Agra, uncle Bal Mukund moved to Delhi. India's national capital was in the throes of a thorough post-Independence shake-up, and the markets were in a state of complete disarray so he went back to the family's abiding passion: bicycles. By this time, he had two sons and six daughters.

After a few years, in the early 1960s, uncle Bal Mukund moved to Ludhiana as well, and set up a factory to manufacture bicycle saddles under the brand name 'Regent'. He never involved himself directly in Hero Cycles, but was always at hand to proffer advice.

Eventually uncle Sadanand, too, was called to Ludhiana. My father had purchased an oxygen gas plant during one of his forays to Germany and this was handed over to his elder brothers. It was set up behind the Hero Cycles facility, to supply Oxygen and Nitrogen to the main Hero Cycles plant. A steel plant now operates out of this facility.

4

Hero Goes National

Ludhiana was abuzz in the autumn of 1968. A city of tents had sprung up on a vast expanse of vacant land, to accommodate over a thousand visitors from out of town. These special guests were Hero dealers, who had been invited to celebrate a new landmark in the history of Hero Cycles. Production figures had crossed 1.25 lakh that year and the company was ready to relocate to its sprawling new facility that had come up on a patch of wilderness adjacent to the Grand Trunk Road. To celebrate this significant milestone, the Munjal brothers decided to felicitate their dealers by hosting an all-India conference.

A convention on this scale was hitherto unheard of and the entire industry was intrigued. Hero dealers from all over the country converged on Ludhiana to take a look inside the heart of a business in which they were all stakeholders. Accommodation was scarce, because hotel capacity was limited, so the brothers decided to put them up in tents. Literally in a matter of days, a sprawling city of tents came up next to the factory.

Hero's range of vehicles, in production and in the planning stage, were on display. Ideas were exchanged, experiences shared and discussions held on best practices and modes of expansion. The Munjals didn't want to make it a purely work trip; they were grateful to their dealers and vendors and wanted them to know it.

The idea was to celebrate big. Then, as now, that meant a live performance by the leading musical artistes of the day. My father and uncles picked each other's brains and drew up a list of potential performers. My father fished out his telephone diary he retained from his days in Bombay, where he had schmoozed with the best and brightest of Bollywood. Uncle Om Prakash reached out to the classical music legends whom he followed with a passion.

My siblings and cousins shared my delight at the prospect of hosting the legendary singers, Mahendra Kapoor and Asha Bhosle. For us, these were names on record sleeves and album covers and disembodied voices emerging from the radio or the phonograph. To see them in the flesh, to hear them perform live, was the most exciting event of our lives. I can only imagine how thrilled our guests must have been, many of whom came from small towns.

These events were to become an established practice and were held to mark any milestone in the family or in the business. Among those who regaled us with their incredible performances over the years were Ustad Allah Rakha, Pandit Ravi Shankar and Hema Malini. We all got our fill of the arts, covering the whole range from classical forms to popular culture. Perhaps that's how my interest in the arts got triggered and led me to set up a foundation dedicated to conserving and developing India's rich legacy of arts.

The idea of celebrating the company's growth with all the stakeholders – employees, vendors and dealers – was in keeping with the Munjal philosophy that they were all part of the Hero family and treated as such.

Uncle Dayanand made it a point to keep track of the senior employees' families and attend all their functions, be it a birth, marriage, death or housewarming. If he could not go, he insisted that at least one member of the family go in his stead. The same courtesy was extended to all Hero vendors and dealers. This emphasis on relationships was the glue that held the entire enterprise together.

Yogesh remembers the time when they were walking across the floor in the factory premises. Uncle Dayanand, as a result of the serious injury he had sustained during the Quetta earthquake, had an awkward gait. One of the workers, a young fellow with a puerile sense of humour, started aping his gait. Yogesh was enraged. The lad's supervisor scolded him severely but Yogesh was not mollified and wanted to throw the boy out of the factory gates and dismiss him peremptorily. Uncle Dayanand intervened, saying, the youngster had been adequately chastened and it was time for him to get back to work.

Later, he explained that the relationship between the employer and employee was a filial one, with both being part of a big family. It was incumbent on the employer to correct a transgression, but throwing out an employee was the last and not the first resort.

Uncle Dayanand also wanted to make the employees as comfortable as possible in their place of work. He insisted on installing a fountain in front of the factory and designed it personally. Long before Feng Shui and Zen became buzzwords, he created a soothing miniature garden centred around a fish pond, fed by a steady trickle of water. Factories in those days tended to be rather utilitarian structures, with no embellishments to cheer the eye, so it attracted no small attention.

* *

On the final day of that first big get-together in 1968, the Munjals decided a little tourism was in order. Their guests were split into two groups, one of which would go to Amritsar and the other to the Bhakra Nangal dam.

Uncle Dayanand had supervised the arrangements for the mega-meet personally and was tired, but insisted on accompanying the group which opted for Bhakra Nangal. Their bus broke down en route. My uncle got off the bus and joined the other passengers in their efforts to push the bus, in the hope that it would start. For a man with a known cardiac condition, it was not a wise decision. Besides, he had injured himself a few days earlier, while lifting a heavy piece of equipment in one of the Hero godowns. The exertion put further stress on his already over-burdened heart and he collapsed on the road.

After returning to Ludhiana, uncle Dayanand was asked by our family to slow down yet he insisted on supervising the construction of offices at the Rockman factory, an ancillary unit that the Munjals were setting up to integrate their bicycle operations. As a concession to his well-wishers, he told Yogesh to take charge of the work on the upper floor, while he oversaw the work on the ground floor.

The cumulative stress was the last straw. In a matter of a fortnight, he suffered a cardiac arrest and our beloved uncle Dayanand passed away. The overarching father figure on whose wisdom and unfailing affection our entire family had relied, had left us and it was difficult to fill the vacuum. I was very young at the time, but I remember my father and uncles, my mother and my aunts, our neighbours and friends, all struggling to cope with the grief of his passing.

The bereaved brothers resolved not to be defeated by grief. My cousin Vijay took his father's position in the company and was treated on par with his uncles. In later years, every picture of the Munjal patriarchs from those days shows him standing with them, representing his father. The Munjals turned to their business with renewed determination and evolved a long-term expansion strategy.

At this time, the Indian economy was just beginning to emerge from a massive crisis. Two successive monsoon failures in 1965 and 1966 had led to a fall in agricultural output by 17 per cent and foodgrain output by 20 per cent. The inflation rate, hitherto no more than 2 per cent, rose sharply to 12 per cent between 1965 and 1968 and food prices escalated by 20 per cent per annum.

The India-China war of 1962 and the India-Pakistan war of 1965 had necessitated a massive increase in defence expenditure, and the fiscal deficit peaked at 7.3 per cent of the GDP in 1966–67.

The balance of payments situation, fragile since 1956–57, deteriorated further, with foreign exchange reserves (excluding gold) averaging about $340 million between 1964–65 and 1966–67, enough to cover less than two months of imports. The dependence on foreign aid, which had been rising over the first three Plan periods,[10] now increased sharply because of the food shortage, as well as the adverse balance of payments.

External assistance, which was 0.86 per cent of Net National Product (NNP) in 1951–52, increased to 3.8 per cent in 1965–66.

Amortization and interest payments as a percentage of exports (debt service ratio) rose sharply from 0.8 per cent up to a whopping 27.8 in 1966–67.

Despite the depressing macro-economic indicators, the market for bicycles continued to grow and Hero Cycles kept pace with it. In fact, 1968 was a landmark in the company's history with Hero Cycles shifting from its earlier premises in Ludhiana's Miller Ganj, the site of an old flour mill, to a vast stretch of wilderness on GT Road on which my father fulfilled his vision of building a world-scale factory The factory site and its surrounding region would come to be known as Hero Nagar and developed as an industrial hub.

My father completely shouldered the responsibility of setting up the new factory in what was then the middle of nowhere! He insisted on the sparse location, the massive acreage and the scale of the shopfloor.

---

[10] Economic planning in India was done across five-year spans from the 1950s to 2014.

He also decided on the layout and oversaw the construction. He made sure there was plenty of natural light and ventilation, a rarity at the time.

Hero Cycles operated like a number of mini-factories working in parallel. Each division had a manager who oversaw supply of raw materials, manufacturing and despatch. A large blackboard at one end of the shop floor was constantly updated with the latest production figures. The bicycles were shipped in CKD (completely knocked down) kits, which were then assembled by the dealers at their end.

Many years later, another successful entrepreneur from Ludhiana would recall a visit to the Hero factory. His name was Sunil Bharti Mittal and he wrote to my father on his ninetieth birthday, saying: 'I can never forget when you took me to your shop floor. How deeply impressed I was as I admired gleaming and spotless machinery. It was unthinkable to imagine an engineering shop floor that could be kept so pristine. Only realized that I had seen such plants in Japan, never in India. Obviously, you were so ahead of your times.'

* *

After his trip to Germany, my father came into his own. He nurtured his newly formed transnational relationships zealously. His most prized possession was a small telephone diary, in which he had entered the names and numbers of all his associates and friends. For the next decade, he travelled the world in search of fresh opportunities, new ideas, the latest technology and the most modern equipment. His head was always abuzz with ideas for adding value and pushing growth and ambitions of building new factories. Creating a legacy, as it were.

Uncle Om Prakash always said that my father was never designed for 'small things' and needed to fly at a great height. 'A man like him cannot derive much satisfaction from the kind of work we were doing in the early days.' My father was irrepressible, always imagining the next big thing and thinking on a global scale.

He was also tasked with the delicate business of liaising with government officials. The nanny state of the 1960s was quite capable of stifling a business if a senior babu was displeased. All businesses ensured an amicable working relationship with the government, and my father, with his warm and expansive personality, was ideally suited to the task of external stakeholder management.

By this time, Hero Cycles' storied supply chain and dealership network were in place. Both were built on the Munjal imperative – the personal touch. Uncle Om Prakash not only knew each of his dealers by name, but was familiar with their circumstances and life stories. A Hero dealer could call him at any time of the day or night, or turn to him for help in times of trouble and be assured of getting it.

Once, uncle Om Prakash heard that one of his dealers had been robbed and the safe in his house had been emptied, so he went to the unfortunate gentleman's house and found him crying helplessly. 'What happened?' he asked. The poor dealer wept even harder. Uncle Om Prakash asked him to stop crying, because he had not lost anything. The man was dumbfounded. It turned out that my uncle had found out exactly how much had been stolen and had credited the matching amount to the dealer's bank account, without telling him.

On another occasion, a truck en route to a dealership developed a fault while on the road and went up in flames, along with the entire consignment. Technically, once the truck had left the factory, it was no longer Hero's responsibility, but that wasn't how uncle Om Prakash looked at it. He asked his right-hand man Tirath Ram, asked him to investigate, and soon it became apparent that the truck and the consignment had been incinerated.

Without a word to the dealer, a brand new truck was despatched, with a fresh consignment. There are many such stories, some of which will be related later in the book. The legendary commitment and loyalty of Hero's dealers can be attributed in a large measure to uncle Om Prakash's considerate and large-hearted approach to business partners.

Hero's unique production schema – Just In Time or JIT – was the result of a peculiar set of circumstances. The Munjal brothers, irked by the artificial limits on production imposed by supply constraints, had laid the foundations of robust ancillaries. As mentioned previously, bicycle parts were imported through the erstwhile agency houses and distributed through a quota system. For example, if you had 1,000 hubs for the wheels, you could make 500 bicycles and that was that.

The Munjal brothers went around to their family and friends, suggesting that they set up component manufacturing businesses and become suppliers to Hero Cycles. The understanding was that Hero would not fund or run the business, but by working in synergy, everyone would benefit. There were three outcomes. First, it created the world's most efficient supply chain. Second, it became the trigger for the largest concentration of bicycle part manufacturers in the world. Third, it allowed Hero to create the famous zero-inventory manufacturing system (JIT).

Our supply chain delivered exactly as much as was required on a particular day and not one component more. We never offered an advance, but ensured that our vendors received their payments without delay. To Bhagatji, our chief cashier, goes the credit for creating Hero's formidable reputation for prompt payments, so much so that vendors and dealers would clear their credits, even before they received their cheques from the company.

It became an article of faith with them; on Saturday afternoon, come hail or sunshine, they would walk up to Bhagatji's window between 2 p.m. and 5 p.m. and pick up their cheques. Anyone who failed to do so, would find his cheque in the mail.

We had no warehouses for incoming or outgoing goods, because we couldn't afford to have our capital locked up. Component supplies arrived between 10 a.m. and 8 p.m., some every couple of hours and others every few days. The finished bicycles would be dispatched to dealers on a daily basis and after 6 p.m., not a single bicycle could be found on the premises. Just as vendors took it for granted that their payments would be made on Saturday, the dealers were assured that the cycles would reach their outlets without delay. At the same time, they knew that they would not receive goods unless earlier payments were cleared. Most of them would make advance payments, to ensure an uninterrupted supply.

For an engineering company to operate with negative working capital was a first. Thanks to advances from dealers, we could pay suppliers on time without having to borrow and we always had deposits in the banks. What had started as a compulsion because money was tight, became our strength. It was almost picture perfect. We designed all our subsequent companies on the lean manufacturing principle, which was regarded as a characteristic of South East Asian businesses. So,when the Japanese partnered with Hero in the 1980s, our systems resonated with their 'Muda-Mura-Muri', popularly known as the Toyota 3M model.

The 'vertically disintegrated' production system was possible because of close engagement with vendors. They were always treated with respect and affection, but the Munjals knew that in order to ensure loyalty, their profitability had to be ensured. Pricing was transparent and payments, as mentioned earlier, were made on the dot.

The proximity was geographical as well as metaphorical. Having vendors close to the main plant contributed to efficiency and productivity. Early on, a vendor development section had been put in place and the precise specifications of each component were given to the vendors, along with training on parts development.

The gauges used by the manufacturers were produced in Hero's own tool room and were periodically recalibrated in the interests of standardization and consistent quality. If any of the suppliers had a problem, Hero engineers would be despatched to resolve it. Once a year, a workshop would be held for all the vendors. The brothers were constantly looking for innovation and process upgrades, which would be passed on to the vendors and my father's maxim was, 'There is always room for improvement.'

The first ancillary to be set up was Rockman Cycle Industries, which produced bicycle chains and hubs. Union Minister Manubhai Shah was invited to inaugurate the new premises. The next was Munjal Gases, established in 1962, with a view to ensuring a stable supply of industrial gases to the main plant. It was followed by Hero Rims in 1969 and Highway Cycles in 1971.

Hero companies were trend setters in a variety of ways. The fact that capital was limited engendered an impulse towards cost-cutting and greater efficiency and a lean system that was followed across all companies. The family owned units looked to the mothership for help in sourcing raw materials, technical guidance and machinery, but not for capital.

As Hero's cash flows improved, the brothers also made it a practice to extend financial support to dealers and suppliers to meet working capital requirements, on a case by case basis. In the early days, access to institutional finance was limited and interests rates were exhorbitant. By giving channel partners a hand in times of difficulty or crisis, the Munjals won a lot of goodwill and cemented loyalties, which helped them craft together a stable and sustainable business.

* *

The growth trajectory continued into the 1970s. Soon after Highway Cycles, Majestic Auto was established in 1972, to produce bicycle spokes. It was followed a year later by Majestic Gears, essentially a rim-making division. In 1981, Munjal Casting was added to the Hero bouquet of companies.

Highway Cycles, with Ramanji at the helm, went on to become the world's second-largest freewheel manufacturer; in fact, in later years, it began modifying existing machines to make special-purpose machines for the manufacture of not just cycle components, but also mopeds and motorcycles.

Highway Cycles became the group's hub for engineering talent, ideas and innovation, where workflows and production cycles were developed to improve operational efficiencies across the group. To give an example, when four rotary milling machines were built at Highway Cycles these helped phase out forty older machines; what's more, the price of the rotary milling machine was just half that of the older machine!

By 1975, Hero Cycles – some two decades after the first experimental bicycle rolled out – had become the largest manufacturer of bicycles in India, producing half a million cycles a year. It had overtaken Atlas, its main competitor.

Of course, one of the big turning points for the volume growth in Hero Cycles and thus in all the bicycle component businesses, was providential. In the 1970s, there was a workers strike in Atlas Cycles, which was then the largest player in the industry. According to elders who were with Hero Cycles at the time, the strike lasted for a while, and also coincided with the peak season of the bicycle industry, prompting Atlas Cycle dealers to rush to Hero Cycles to procure their supplies. Once they entered into this relationship with Hero Cycles, they got to experience our way of doing business in terms of fairness, timely supplies, consistent quality and timely payment. From this point on, their relationships with Hero became permanent, and this put Hero Cycles on a continuous growth path.

Like other iconic brands established in the 1960s and 1970s, Hero became synonymous with the product. If 'Godrej' was the default term for steel cupboards, 'Colgate' for toothpaste and 'Dalda' for hydrogenated vegetable oil, Hero meant a bicycle.

The humble bicycle had come to reflect the aspirations and circumstances of the common man. The first thing he purchased after providing for food, shelter and clothing, was a bicycle. It was transformative, in that it provided mobility, which in turn brought the freedom to pursue economic opportunities. My father would often say that the number of bicycles sold was an accurate indicator of the health of the economy! The bicycle also became an integral part of weddings in rural India. Gifting a 'Hero' as part of a bride's dowry became de rigeur.

Exports had been initiated as early as in 1963, when Hero sent its first consignment overseas to Indonesia. The government offered incentives for exports, but in the inhibiting business atmosphere of the time, this involved negotiations at multiple levels of bureaucracy, in order to secure that all-important export licence. The Munjal brothers managed to pull it off, thanks to their people skills.

Of course, I don't want to give the impression that the Hero story was a sanguine fairy tale; ours was a normal business family with the usual issues and challenges.

As the business of Hero Cycles began to grow along with that of our bicycle component firms, we faced newer hurdles. Despite amazing relationships, we had our share of strikes at Hero-promoted bicycle component firms, such as Rockman Industries and Highway Cycles.

Since these companies were governed in a style that was bigger and better governed than small component firms, their cost structures became higher than some of the competitors. Despite being clearly better and having more consistent quality, sourcing components from our family owned firms at competitive prices became a challenge.

After many heated debates and discussions, when it became increasingly clear that Hero Cycles would not be able to procure at the prices being offered by our own component companies, especially at a time when they (our component companies) already had a labour strike going on, we took a tough decision to shut down the bicycle component business units. In subsequent years, of course, these component firms evolved and became world-class auto component businesses in their own right.

* *

The 1970s were a golden period for Indian industry in terms of a growing overseas market. China was still a few decades away from establishing itself as the manufacturing base for the world. It was only natural that Ludhiana's industries would power exports, shipping hosiery, wool and cycle parts to Europe, Russia and South East Asia.

By 1977, Hero had a full-fledged and thriving exports division. Bicycles and their components were already being exported to developing nations like Indonesia, Kenya, Iran and Iraq. With the growth of exports, the Munjals realized that their capacity would have to expand to keep pace with the demand. Accordingly, a separate unit was initiated to tackle the additional volumes. My cousin Vijay, our late uncle Dayanand's eldest son, was asked to supervise the expansion.

Ramanji had also joined the family business by this time and helped Vijay expand exports, particularly those of the freewheels now being manufactured by the ancillaries, to Europe. It was the thin end of the wedge; within a few years, Ramanji's uncompromising insistence on meeting international quality standards had gained the trust of European buyers and Cycle freewheels made by Hero ancillaries made their debut across Europe, expanding a market that was previously virtually inaccessible to firms from the developing world.

To ensure that exports could become a viable and sustainable proposition, a dedicated export unit in Baroda, Gujarat Cycles, was set up in 1985, within reach of the coast to facilitate quick access to ports.

While Hero never considered itself a global enterprise, in many ways it has been global for a long time and some of the initiatives even predate the current practices of global enterprises. For example, a bicycle plant was set up in Sri Lanka in the 1970s which was then handed over to the partner or the customer to run. Similar initiatives were also undertaken in other countries of Africa and Latin America.

This created a unique ecosystem where Hero Cycles not only supplied the plant and the know-how for manufacture of bicycles, but also had a business where components were supplied on an ongoing basis. This and the other outreach into both the developing and developed world allowed Hero Cycles and the component manufacturing entities in the group (Highway, Rockman, etc.,) to supply bicycles and components to more than ninety countries.

Many experts will tell you the capacity of a machine determines the ability of an enterprise to grow; but one of the strengths of Hero was its complete ignorance of these theoretical limitations. There are hundreds of examples, where we used the machines to produce many times more than the rated capacity set by the machine manufacturer.

We were never really burdened by limitations. As an organization, many records were broken and milestones were set without thinking of these as something special; nor did we see limitations as constraints. This came from a lack of exposure to global enterprises and we were simply charting a path without following anyone's footsteps.

A number of people played a key role in shaping Hero's character and we encountered them during our internships. I have already mentioned Bhagatji (more on him in a subsequent chapter).

All of us remember Sadhu Singh, who ran the Hero Cycles canteen. His mouth-watering *samosas*, stuffed with boiled peas, linger in our collective memory. At 11 a.m. and 3.30 p.m. every day, a canteen trolley laden with tea, samosas and biscuits would trundle through the factory. Everyone was served. Sadhu Singh was unflappable; he could whip up a meal for twenty guests in a jiffy.

Then there was S.K. Mehta who had joined Hero straight out of law college in the 1950s and looked after our legal affairs. Our head of finance was S.C. Chhabra and both my father and I had the privilege of working with him. At Rockman was the imperturbable Satpal, a troubleshooter extraordinaire while Highway Cycles was enriched by the presence of Anand Singh, who had a genius for designing machine tools.

* *

By the early-1970s, my father had begun looking around for the next big thing. As always, he found it. During his visits overseas, he had been introduced to what was essentially a motorized bicycle, or 'moped'. These feisty little vehicles were tough, fuel-efficient and pocket-friendly. He realized that they had immense potential. Back home, early birds had already jumped into the untapped market for a low-budget, motorized two-wheeler. Pune-based Kinetic

Engineering enjoyed a near-monopoly with their smart and sprightly 50 cc Luna mopeds. TVS from Hosur in Tamil Nadu, was the other first-comer.

In his mind's eye, my father could see a moped trundling over rough village roads, twin canisters of milk balanced on either side of the pillion. Like all peri-urban Indians, he was familiar with the milkman's large aluminum canister from which milk would be measured out *pau* by *pau* (quarter litre). He went from house to house, with the canister firmly secured to the carrier of – you guessed it – a Hero cycle. The milkman, my father's instincts told him, was ready for a seamless transition from a cycle to a moped.

Whither the milkman led, the rest of rural India would follow. My father was right. Rural India had embraced the bicycle with enthusiasm, now it welcomed the moped as a low-budget, all-purpose utility vehicle. Despite being notoriously underpowered (less than 100 cc), it could carry heavy loads and negotiate rough village roads. It was dashing, liberating and agile; it made the rider feel every bit the Hero. Bollywood was relentlessly promoting motorcycles (*Bobby*, 1973 and *Sholay*, 1975) and the much-more affordable moped was the next best thing.

So, when the Indian government, quite open to the idea of modernizing the largely bicycle-centric personal transportation market, issued manufacturing licences for mopeds, the Munjals were enthused. Nevertheless, it required a different approach as bicycles were low-tech and there was need for a technological partner. My father, with his great respect for European engineering, was keen on a foreign collaboration. Off he went to France, to meet with the management of automobile maker Peugeot. Peugeot had launched three 50 cc mopeds between the late 1960s and early 1970s and was a market leader in France. Its two factories at Romily and St. Louis produced 800,000 mopeds a year during this period.

It was a difficult environment for foreign technology agreements. World scooter leader Piaggio had licenced the Vespa to Bajaj Autos in the 1960s, only to have that licence cancelled in 1971, as a result of Prime Minister Indira Gandhi's nationalization agenda. The Monopolies and Restrictive Trade Practices (MRTP) Act was passed in 1969 and 'big' business houses, Bajaj Auto among them, were shackled.

Riding a wave of popularity in the wake of the 1971 India-Pakistan war, she carried her policy forward and by 1974, had nationalized fourteen big banks, as well as general insurance companies and coal mines. Subsequently, the Foreign Exchange Regulations Act (FERA) came into force in 1974 and restricted the operation of foreign companies in India.

When my father met the moped leadership team members at Peugeot they took some convincing, but finally saw the merits in partnering with a strong Indian brand. Delighted with the in-principle agreement, my father returned to India.

Fate and the Indian government had other ideas. We applied for the requisite clearances with great enthusiasm and discovered what the term 'stonewalled' meant. Confronted with a Himalayan pile of paperwork and severe currency restrictions under FERA, the Munjals were brought up short.

Telephone lines between Ludhiana and Paris sizzled with trunk calls as my father tried to find a way out. Without foreign exchange, there was no question of importing technology so the partnership with Peugeot ended even before it could be properly inked. The dreams of collaborating with Peugeot faded, but not through any lack of effort on my father's part.

The environment at the time was certainly hostile to foreign collaboration. Under FERA, global companies with subsidiaries in India had to offer their shares to the public at a fraction of their real value – the price being determined by the Controller of Capital Issues.

Salaries for company executives were capped, despite rampant inflation, and income tax rates were jacked up. If the effect of the wealth tax was taken into account, a well-off individual might find his combined tax burden exceeding his income. Those who wanted to travel out of the country were allowed all of $8 and that too, after negotiating a mile of red tape.

Price controls, on everything from paper to steel, tyres to cement and medicines to cars, resulted in weird distortions. The waiting list for Bajaj scooters was as long as seventeen years at its peak; bridegrooms were enticed into marriage by the promise of a 'Bajaj' as part of the dowry. Black markets thrived and bureaucrats who were entitled to purchase Premier (earlier Fiat) cars, which were in short supply, on a preferential quota, could sell them off after three years at a substantantial profit.

In 1973, private wholesale trade in foodgrain was abolished, a move that many saw as counterproductive and sure enough, food prices soared. These radical steps were attributed to the influence of the Communists, who had supported Indira Gandhi when the Congress split in 1969.

On the political front, Supreme Court judges were superseded in order to handpick a new chief justice. With the ascent of Sanjay Gandhi, the Leftists were sidelined, but the damage had been done and economic growth dipped to 2.5 per cent from 4 per cent, even as inflation exceeded 30 per cent.

Political opposition to the Congress regime gathered force and found a focus in Gandhian socialist leader Jayaprakash Narain. Even as the youth across India flocked to 'JP's' banner, the prime minister's election to the Lok Sabha was declared void by the Allahabad High Court. Opposition to Indira Gandhi intensified as a result and, on 25 June 1975, a state of Emergency was imposed nationwide. A crackdown on civil liberties ensued. The Supreme Court, headed by chief justice A.N. Ray, who was appointed in 1973 by superseding three of his senior colleagues, upheld the power of the state to suspend fundamental rights.

The tumultous politics of the day and the uncertain economic environment would have deterred most businessmen, but my father was determined to forge ahead. His view that India was in dire need of a low-cost and easily accessible alternative to scooters and motorcycles was firmed up. The brothers studied moped designs and concluded that the technology wasn't rocket science, and the moped could be engineered in India with local talent. Of course, it required a mammoth effort. The brothers and their progeny sat down with engineers and artisans to deconstruct the moped and plan its manufacture, component by component.

The first indigenously designed moped, the Hero Majestic, rolled out in 1975. There were glitches aplenty and the design team ironed them out over the next couple of years. It was Majestic Auto that powered the Munjal group into the next phase of growth. The brothers decided to take the company public in 1977, because they needed to raise capital.

The following year, the first Hero Majestic mopeds were on the roads. Riding on the Hero brand (which signified value for money) and its vast sales and distribution network, it made strong strides in the market. By the mid-1980s, the Hero Majestic was a household name, and one of the reasons for this was its competitive price, compared to those offered by Kinetic Engineering (Luna) and Sundaram Clayton (TVS 50).

The Hero Majestic also found great acceptance across the globe: in Africa, North and South America, Europe and the Middle East. Several years down the line, my father's desire for a foreign collaborator in mopeds materialized in the form of a 'light motorcycle'. Steyr Daimler Puch of Austria, founded in 1899 by Johann Puch and a leader in automobiles, bicycles, mopeds, and motorcycles, was happy to share its technical know-how. In 1986, my cousin Pankaj bought three models from them and Hero Motors got off the ground. The products found an export market in West Asia, Bangladesh and Vietnam.

The Hero Puch was a sleek roadster, with actor Aamir Khan as its brand ambassador. When the hit film *Sarfarosh* opened to packed theatres in 1999, my father (then seventy-six) had the satisfaction of seeing Aamir, who played a cop, riding a Hero Puch down the roads of Delhi. The ad copy, a waggish blogger wrote, applied as much to the bike as to Aamir: 'You don't have to be big to pack a powerful punch.'

Puch was a great brand in the moped business and offered quality at affordable prices. In India's challenging terrain – awful roads with lots of sand and dust – it promised and delivered reliability. Puch's technical expertise, though, wasn't matched by its marketing and commercial operations and shortly thereafter, it was sold to Piaggio – which still produces bikes under the Puch brand. At the same time, the entire production line of Puch Maxi Plus was sold to Hero Motors.

The Hero Puch did well from 1988 until 2003, when it was finally laid to rest as customers across India switched to higher powered motorcycles and scooters.

5

The Hero-Honda Partnership

By the year 1981, Hero was a market leader in bicycles and mopeds. Exports had taken off; Hero Cycles had experimented with high-end and complex bicycles for the overseas market, with considerable success. Five companies were up and running and a sixth, Munjal Casting, had been inaugurated.

On the face of it, Hero seemed to be on a strong wicket, but there were rumblings beneath the crust. Moped sales were beginning to falter. The zesty little vehicles had had a good run, but the consumer fad was now over, partly because they tended to break down easily. Unlike bicycles, after-sales service was problematic as not every mechanic could repair them. Also, it was very difficult to ride pillion on the moped, as it was essentially designed for one rider. The great Indian spirit of jugaad could only go so far.

Baulked of a partnership with Peugeot, my father began casting around for other foreign collaborations. With the prescient vision that contributed so much to Hero's success, he wanted to take the company global and that meant a tie-up with a big international brand. He brought up the subject at one of the family's regular informal meetings.

First, he spoke of the necessity of expanding the family business, in tandem with the growth taking place in the country and the increasing aspirations of the people, as a result of the opportunities this progress offered. The Munjal progeny was now grown up and had been placed in various group companies. Educated and forward-looking, they represented a talent pool that could power Hero's growth in the decades to come.

Then, my father pointed to the shift in government policy. The restrictive regime that began in the 1970s was coming to an end. The motorcycle and scooter segments, thanks to FERA, had seen neither new products nor firms entering the market since it was heavily dependent on foreign collaborations.

The pendulum, having reached apogee, had begun its reverse swing. From Emergency (1975–77), through the Janata governments (1977–80) and Indira Gandhi's return to power in 1980, the direction of the government's economic policy gradually began to change. Price controls were lifted, MRTP lost momentum, foreign exchange controls were eased and companies were allowed 'automatic' expansion of capacity. The waiting list for Bajaj scooters eventually disappeared.

Now, foreign collaboration for two-wheelers up to 100 cc had been allowed. This created new opportunities for two-wheeler manufacturers in the motorcycle and scooter segments, opening up avenues for new products, business partners and markets. For the domestic two-wheeler industry, with a market characterized by high demand and low supply, this was good news. The 1980s promised to be a decade of increased production and better quality.

At first, family and friends discouraged my father against pursuing foreign partnerships. Mr Rai recalls, 'There was fear amongst family members that this was going to be a big gamble.' What if they got into a partnership, only to have it fall through? What about money? Building a partnership would require a large infusion of funds, where would it come from?

My father, the dreamer, was undeterred in his search for potential partners. He was determined that Hero would transition from being a bicycle-and-moped manufacturer to a leader in scooters and motorcycles. Ensconced in his office with a notepad and pen, he shot off handwritten letters to automotive majors in Europe and elsewhere. He researched the global scenario, deploying his transnational network of contacts. As my brother Suman observes, 'He was brilliant with his homework. He had meticulously scanned and gauged companies that were looking to enter the Indian market.'

He homed in on Japan. Indeed, all automotive manufacturers were looking eastwards. Honda, one of the world's largest automotive companies (the third largest in Japan) and the top producer of two-wheelers, had a number of offerings with an engine capacity of 100 cc and less. This was exactly what my father wanted, to facilitate a seamless transition for customers, from cycles and mopeds to fuel-efficient and low-maintenance motorcycles and scooters. Honda had, in fact, already advertised for an Indian partner, as the paucity of vehicles in India and the sheer size of the market made the country an attractive proposition. My father was convinced he could get Honda on board, provided he could get into their boardroom for a meeting.

The family was sceptical about Hero's chances and understandably so. Honda had received more than 140 applications, including those from companies with financial and industrial muscle, several orders of magnitude higher than Hero's. '*Arre, humare saath kyon karenge,* Tata *aur baaki badi companiyon ke saath* foreign partnerships *hongi*' (Why would they go with us, they would prefer Tata or some other big company), was uncle Om Prakash's view. Indeed, Honda's short list of twenty-two comprised a veritable who's who of industrial houses in the country.

Honda was incorporated in 1948, but its roots lay in the pre-Second World War economic expansion of Japan. Its founder, Soichiro Honda, whom my father had the pleasure of meeting in the early days, when the joint venture was being inked, started with a bicycle repair shop and went on to become an accomplished auto mechanic. He supplied pistons to Toyota and, working with a staff of just twelve people out of a small shack, he experimented with motorcycles. The first product, dubbed 'Dream' rolled out in 1949 and so popular did it prove to be that by 1964, Honda was the world's largest motorcycle manufacturer. The rest is history.

The up-from-the-bootstraps story resonated with our family's own evolution from bicycle parts to bicycles and mopeds. The first meeting with Honda in Japan happened quite by chance. In the early eighties, my father was on a trip to Japan to buy machine parts; Hero's agent in Japan was Mr Wasu, a resident of Kobe in Osaka. My father told Mr Wasu about Honda's interest in entering India with a local partner; a number of Indian companies had already started approaching Honda and my father wanted to know if he, too, could meet someone of influence in the company.

Mr Wasu then spoke to a colleague of his, who fortuitously knew a high-ranking executive who had joined Honda recently. After a few phone calls, it turned out that the Honda contact, Koji Wanaka, was the official who was tasked by the Honda management to explore the automotive major's entry into India. A meeting at the Honda headquarters was set up. Mr Wanaka, incidentally, later came to India to head up Honda's scooter venture with Kinetic Engineering, which ran parallel to Hero Honda.

My father, with Yogesh in tow, departed for Japan buoyant, expectant and determined.

As Mr Wasu was Hero's representative in the island nation, the Munjals expected him to receive them at Tokyo's Narita airport, which had opened just five years earlier amidst tumultuous public protests over acquisition of land for the airport.

Mr Wasu or his sons Ronnie and Manjit were nowhere in sight when the Munjals emerged through the arrival gates. When they called him, he told them to take a bus to their hotel. A bus? They hadn't expected an Indian-style welcome, with warm hugs, marigold garlands and a chauffeur-driven car, but a bus was underwhelming. 'Wasu told us taxis were avoidable because of the very high fares. He also said that in Japan, even directors and chairmen of major companies used public transport, like buses and trains. So we went to the hotel by bus and everything was an experience,' Yogesh remembers. They had some trouble finding the hotel because there were two in the same area with almost identical names and a friendly receptionist directed them to the correct location. Their first couple of hours in Tokyo had been an adventure.

Japan was a culture shock. With a bird's-eye view of the Imperial Palace, they had a ringside seat to the holiday-filled Golden Week gala and celebrations to mark the late Showa Emperor's birthday. The Munjals had never seen such a disciplined crowd.

Yogesh was impressed by the thoughtfulness of the Japanese, who had ensured that the Munjals were invited to all the India-related events in Tokyo. The State Bank of India (SBI) was celebrating its anniversary and the SBI's Ludhiana Branch had already informed its counterpart in Japan that the Munjals were in Tokyo. The invitation cards for the bank's anniversary party were awaiting them at the reception, when they checked into the hotel.

'The party was to be held the next evening at 7 p.m. We decided, as was customary in Ludhiana, to join them at around 8:30 pm. But Mr Wasu told us this was unacceptable. If the invite said 7 p.m., we would have to reach on the dot. We were sceptical and decided to stretch it a bit, to 7.10 p.m. To our surprise, everybody was already in the room and seated!' said Yogesh.

The Japanese mode of doing business was, at least prima facie, vastly different from the easygoing Indian style. The fact that they had arrived at dinner ten minutes late, they discovered, was interpreted as a lack of interest. For a couple of days, they were occupied with meetings with bicycle parts suppliers, before they connected with Honda.

One morning, their taxi was stuck in a traffic jam. The driver suggested they take the train so that they could make it in time for their appointment and dropped them off at a railway station. 'We were shocked. In India, we hadn't come across a taxi guy who would give up his earnings and tell us to take public transport,' Yogesh told me.

The first meeting between Honda officials, my father and Yogesh took place in the conference room, and my father stood out like a beacon. Everyone present wore dark suits. He had opted for beige. At the head of the table was Koji Wanaka, wearing a black suit and an impassive countenance.

The faces around him were deadpan, but there was a faint hint of bonhomie in the air, which buoyed the Munjals' confidence. My father started to introduce himself, but the Honda team gently intervened and told him there was no need. 'They already had a detailed dossier on Hero and the Munjal family. They had researched the Indian business scenario, the state of road infrastructure, climatic conditions and the legal framework,' recalls Yogesh.

* *

Honda and Hero eventually came together, despite their diverse backgrounds, because of the affinities they shared, and this became quite apparent when Honda began its due diligence in the early 1980s. To begin with, a large team of people arrived to explore Hero's operations. Another followed, then yet another. My brother Suman recalls, 'Their teams would come, visit all the factories and take notes. After a few weeks, the second-level team would come and try to understand the people and the work culture. They would meet with the workers and managers over several days.' The Japanese teams, armed with black notebooks (there were no tablets in those days) and cameras, became a familiar sight at our plants and dealerships.

Mr S.K. Rai came on board at this time. A senior executive at Guest Keen Williams, he was lured to Hero by my father. He recalls those early years, 'In the office where I sat, everybody's surname was Munjal, which was very confusing for the Japanese, but they eventually managed to identify the decision-makers.'

The Hero teams, for their part, patiently heard out the Japanese, tried to understand their requirements and incrementally made progress. Having agreed to take the plunge, the family was now beginning to believe that they just might beat bigger companies to the punch.

My father instinctively knew that by merely looking at the books and gauging technical know-how and operational capacity wouldn't satisfy the Japanese. Their unstated concern would be Hero's management systems and industrial relations. How they – the 'Hero family' – presented themselves, in the face of Honda's minute scrutiny, was of paramount importance. He was also aware that Honda had sought detailed feedback from dealers, suppliers, customers, bankers and others.

Honda shortlisted ten contenders, then five and then two (the other being the Firodia group). After three years of due diligence, Honda appeared satisfied with Hero's work culture and ethic, which probably came closest to that of the Japanese. At Hero, as in Japan, our companies recruited and retained the best talent by offering superior benefits and lifetime job security. In fact, when senior executives retired, many would find roles at our schools or colleges or other socially oriented projects. Many would try and ensure that their children or children's children found a place in the Hero Group.

Hero had always respected depth of knowledge, discipline, dedication and efficiency among its staffers, as did Honda. This, in addition to Hero's customer-oriented approach, was the deal-maker.

When we were selected by Honda as one of their partners, we asked why they had decided to go with a comparatively small company. We were given not one but several reasons. We were told that the size of the partner was not important, its potential was. In fact, one of the senior Honda officials, in his conversations with my father just before the joint venture agreement was signed, asked: 'Can you help us become the leader in this industry, in India?' My father said he couldn't guarantee this, but he would try his best.

The Honda officials also told us the similarity in work culture was another major factor. When they had walked onto the shop floor, not one worker stopped to look at them. So focused were they on the task at hand that there was no room for curiosity. They did not glance, much less stare, at the foreigners.

The Honda officials were also impressed by the way we treated our employees. They saw the concept of lifetime employment, which is a common phenomenon in Japan, and which existed in India only in the Tata Group and in Hero.

Honda officials also told us they had not seen such commitment to productivity anywhere.

'Each time we come back to visit you, you rediscover yourself, in terms of machine, layouts and tooling. Your obsession with raising productivity is quite unique,' a senior official told my father.

He added that he hadn't seen anyone treat and work with suppliers the way we did, and said a similar culture existed in Japan, where the company and the vendors worked in collaboration, and shared the benefits of continuous improvement.

The Japanese were obviously profoundly impressed with Hero's JIT manufacturing principle, which they hadn't expected to see in India. Frugal engineering, as far as they were concerned, was a uniquely far East Asian concept and here was an Indian company that had invented it all on its own. Of course, JIT was enabled by the speed and efficiency of the highly trained workers. The Japanese were also surprised at Hero's ability to administer a large workforce and manage stocks and accounting, without computerization.

Another factor was the visible respect displayed by workers towards my father and uncles. If they happened to pass by a worker in the corridor, he would immediately touch their feet in the Indian tradition of respect. The Japanese were impressed, as there would obviously be less possibility of a labour problem in such a set-up!

* *

In 1983, the year the internet was born, Honda invited my father to Japan for a final meeting. That was the year that the Indian government permitted joint ventures in the two-wheeler sector, as my father had anticipated.

Draft agreements on the proposed joint venture had been exchanged previously. My older brothers, Ramanji and Pawan, were actively involved in the project from the very beginning, right from the negotiation stage. Amit Chaturvedi, who joined the company around that time would later say, 'When I came on board, the joint venture agreement with Honda had still not been signed. The draft of the joint venture used to come from abroad. I was told that it was seen by family members and sent back to Japan with changes; there was a lot of back and forth. It was top secret.'

Amit recalled his interview with my father. 'I was interviewed for the job of project manager for the Hero Honda Motorcycle project in June 1983. Ramanji interviewed me, found me okay, and told me I would have to meet his father. The meeting was set up at the Hero Cycles office on Asaf Ali Road. It was a very hot day ... Chairman Saab came in around 1 p.m. wearing a light grey suit. As soon as he came in, he took off his shoes. He asked a lot of questions, especially about my experience of working with the Japanese on a joint venture. By this time, the peon came in and asked Chairman Saab about his lunch. He ordered a south Indian lunch.' A short while later, as the interview ended, Amit Chaturvedi got up to leave, but my father asked him to sit down and share his lunch. Chairman Saab had no airs about him, recalled Amit.

A three-member team led by my father left for Tokyo. My oldest brother, Ramanji and Amit Chaturvedi, accompanied him. Describing the trip, Amit said, 'Ramanji, Brijmohanji and I went to Japan in October 1983. Ramanji was keen that I go, even though Chairman Saab was a little hesitant, but he went along with Ramanji's view.'

At precisely 2.30 p.m. on the following day, the Hero team sat across the table from the Honda representatives. Simultaneously, the family got together in the conference room at their headquarters in Ludhiana. Telecommunications in India had improved to the point that they could monitor events from 5,850 miles away.

Honda had a surprise in store. They told the Hero team that they were ready for a joint venture in motorcycles. At the same time, they would also be entering into a joint venture with the Firodia group to manufacture scooters. The Hero team's jaws dropped. They had come to discuss a venture for scooters, but now were being offered motorcycles! For a few stunned moments, my father stared at the Honda representatives. Then he turned his head to look at Ramanji, who appeared imperturbable, as if unaffected by the astonishing news. He caught our father's eye and almost imperceptibly inclined his head towards the door.

My father got the message and requested the Japanese to excuse them so that they could discuss the matter. The Hero team left the room because they needed time to absorb the implications of Honda's offer. My father called up the family in Ludhiana, who he knew would be waiting anxiously by the telephone. They were bewildered. 'How can we produce motorcycles? People in India want scooters,' observed uncle Om Prakash.

This was uncharted territory and the Munjals had no idea whether motorcycles had any major market potential. After protracted discussions over the telephone all through the afternoon and early evening, they were no nearer to reaching a decision. At this point, my father's instincts took over. He knew that the family's appetite for risk was limited, but if he wanted a collaboration with Honda, it was time to take another leap of faith. Infusing as much confidence in his voice as possible, he declared: 'Let's do this. *Dekhi jayegi*. Cycle *aur* moped *banayi hai, yeh bhi bana lenge*' (Whatever happens, we'll see. We've made cycles and mopeds, we'll manage this as well).

The decision was taken and it was yet another turning point for the Hero Group. The family faced a decisive moment, as it was a big investment for a company of Hero's size, the elders were determined to make it work.

Honda later explained their decision. Their teams had been impressed by Hero's engineering capability and had chosen to partner with the group because they saw scale. Yes, it was an unexplored market for Honda, but with a strong partner, they were convinced that their motorcycles could make a mark in India. None of the existing players, although admittedly strong brands, possessed the combination of quality, economy, fuel-efficiency, distribution network and after-sales service that a Hero-Honda JV could potentially bring. India's rapid increase in population was bound to be matched by an exponential growth in demand. If Hero was making a leap of faith, so was Honda.

At the negotiating table, my father – his convivial and pleasant persona notwithstanding – proved to be a tough cookie. He focused on micro-details. Amit would later comment that he believed the granular approach was deliberate. My father was deeply aware that Hero was on the brink of a great opportunity; at the same time, he wanted to ensure that Honda did not walk away with additional advantages because of its iconic stature. Amit recalled that he and Ramanji had to at times convince my father that some level of give and take was necessary. They would call for a break and hold rapid-fire discussions in Hindi and Punjabi.

Honda first offered a CD 90, which was then very popular in Pakistan and a few other Asian markets, on the assumption that India's market was similar. But my father insisted on a bigger frame and a bigger seat, so that two people could sit comfortably and ride safely. The idea of the motorcycle as a single-rider vehicle, as compared to a scooter which was a vehicle for two, had to change. He also wanted a sari guard, because he imagined women riding pillion. He made it clear to Honda that he wanted the CD 100.

He was also insistent on fuel economy: the vehicle would have to deliver 100 km to a litre. A long argument ensued and the Japanese held that it was impossible for a 100 cc engine to give 100 km per litre (kmpl), at best they could manage 65 kmpl.

My father stuck to his guns. The engineering and R&D teams were summoned and, finally, after much wrangling, they compromised on 80 kmpl!

My father was dogged in other ways as well. He insisted on vegetarian Indian meals, which meant that the Honda officials had to find Indian restaurants. He didn't like tea with powdered milk, so fresh milk had to be procured. Amit said he later realized that these moves were tactical: 'His very tenacity won him a lot of respect from the Japanese. I had negotiated with the Japanese during the Escorts JV, but I had not seen them show as much respect for Indians as they had for Chairman Saab or Lal San (a honorary Japanese title they used for my father my father was known) ... they had figured that he was the driving force behind Hero and could help them succeed in India.'

For ten whole days, they remained in Tokyo, seeing very little other than the walls of conference rooms. They went through the agreement line by line, full stop by full stop, comma by comma and even held discussions on whether a certain word should be in upper or lower case.

The JV agreement between Hero and Honda was signed on 24 December 1983 and a week later, the Memorandum of Agreement was done and dusted. Off went Ramanji, Pawan (some years out of engineering college in Kurukshetra) and Amit to the Registrar of Companies, to submit the documents. Hero Honda Motors Limited officially came into being on 19 January 1984. The partners would each contribute 26 per cent to equity and Hero Honda Motors (HHM) would pay Honda a technical fee and royalty. A whale had partnered with a sprat, but the latter, it would later emerge, was the smartest fish in the waters.

India won the Hockey World Cup only once, in 1975, and Hero Cycles was the first to fete the victorious team when it returned to India from Kuala Lumpur. Each member of the team was presented with a bicycle, which during that era was a treasured possession.

As bicycles in India are a popular mode of family or goods transport, they need to be sturdy. Hero Cycles ensured this by conducting extensive load testing under all conditions, right from the early days.

My father loved cars and driving them fast. He acquired his first car during his early days in Bombay (now Mumbai).

My father and Uncle Om Prakash with Prime Minister P.V. Narasimha Rao and Dr Manmohan Singh, who together crafted the 1991 economic reforms that transformed India.

My parents with my eldest brother Ramanji in Bombay, where my father lived from 1949 to 1951 and started a business in diesel engine parts.

My father at his work desk in Quetta, Baluchistan (now in Pakistan), where he worked as a clerk. He was the first among his brothers to receive a salary from the British ordnance factory, instead of getting a daily wage.

Mother Teresa receiving a donation from my father with grace. In business and in life he was careful with money, but always liberal when it came to supporting causes.

My father receiving the Padma Bhushan Award from President Dr A.P.J. Abdul Kalam in 2005. He received many awards in his lifetime, but this was amongst the ones he cherished the most.

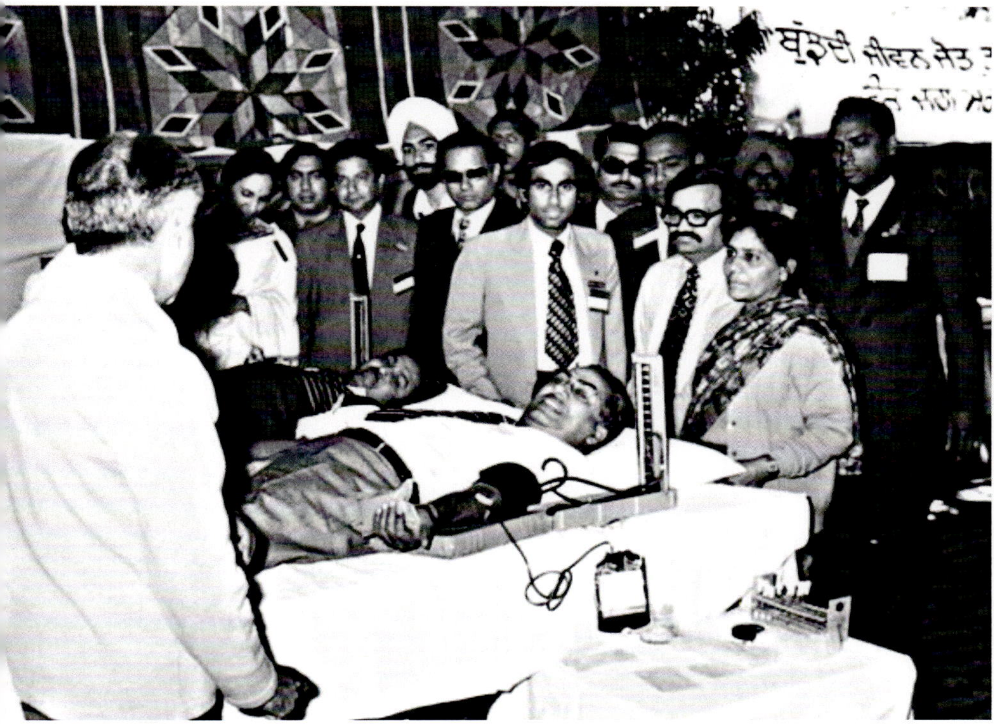

My father was an active Rotarian and donated blood on several occasions: at times for company employees in need.

At the beginning of every speech or before he accepted an award, my father would invariably thank the Almighty for his good fortune and express gratitude to his family.

My father with his close German friend Ernst Mann, who, as my father said, taught him his first lessons on negotiating and buying the best machines and equipment.

A rare picture from pre-partition India, with my father on his way to work in Kamalia (now in Pakistan). I wonder which bicycle he used to ride!

'his rotary milling machine was indigenously developed by master craftsmen at Highway Cycles to make freewheels. It created a new paradigm for efficacy and helped speed up production significantly. Our homegrown creative engineers carefully studied standard machines and improved the throughput, quality and efficiency in innovative ways.

My father with his business rival Rahul Bajaj and the late foreign minister Sushma Swaraj, receiving the Ernst & Young Entrepreneur of the Year Award. Mr Bajaj referred to my father as his 'guru', while the minister called him 'bade bhaisahab' (elder brother).

An early picture of the Hero Cycles Founders' Day, when my father, uncles and senior management staff personally served workers their lunch as part of the celebrations.

Hero Cycles was one of the first companies in India to arrange performances by Hindi film stars. Geeta Dutt, a prominent playback singer, performed at the first big dealers' meet in 1968.

The cult following that cricket today enjoys may have some of its roots in Hero's strong support to he sport in its early days. Here the Indian team, which won the 1993 Hero Cup against South Africa in the last over, poses with the company's management. The umbilical link with sports continues.

The first we heard about Hero Cycles being the largest global manufacturer was when my uncle was shown the Japan Bicycle Press publication featuring the ten largest bicycle makers in the world, with Hero's name right at the top. It then made its way into the Guinness Book of World Records as the largest bicycle maker and stayed there for many years until its removal due to excessive repetition.

My father and brother Pawan proudly pose in front of India Gate in New Delhi, as Hero Honda becomes the world's largest two-wheeler manufacturer in 2001.

A rare occasion to get all the members of the Munjal family involved in the various companies of the then Hero Group on the Hero Cycles lawns in the 1980s.

Members of the Indian and Japanese management celebrate the production of the ten millionth Hero Honda bike, the first Indian auto company to reach this milestone.

The Hero Majestic moped being assembled at the Ludhiana factory. After a venture with a leading foreign partner fell through, the Munjals decided to develop the entire technology indigenously – from sourcing of components to final assembly – everything was made in India, an incredible feat in the 1970s.

Mahendra Kapoor, the legendary playback singer, performed at the 1968 dealers' convention. It was the first private sector convention of its size and scale anywhere in India. Tents the size of a small city came up in the middle of Ludhiana to accommodate hundreds of dealers, and they were personally looked after by the top management of Hero Cycles.

Family members with one of our spiritual gurus, Anand Swamiji. Members of the Munjal family are practising Arya Samajis; havans and social service are still an integral part of our life.

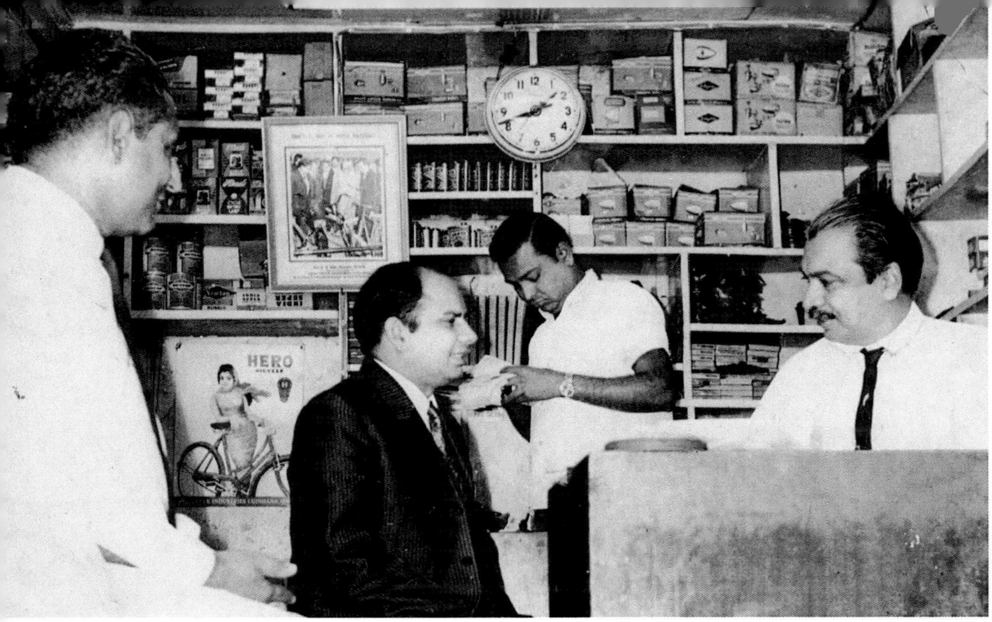

One of the main reasons behind the success of Hero was a result of the personal connect that my father and uncles shared with channel partners. Here, uncle Om Prakash (in a dark suit) is seen with a dealer in Ahmedabad during one of his visits.

Uncle Om Prakash poses with some of the early Hero Cycle dealers in Uttar Pradesh. When Hero Cycles was a fledgling company trying to compete with established players, some of these dealers took a leap of faith and placed orders with us. Today, these relationships have become multi-generational. This picture has two of the oldest dealers from Kanpur and Lucknow on the extreme left.

Hero Cycles was one of the early adopters of robotics and conveyorized mass material movemer technology in the manufacturing assembly line; this was one of the many factors that impressec Honda when they came for their initial visit.

A special picture of all the six Munjal brothers and their brother-in-law from the 1950s. *Sitting (L-R):* Dayanand, Sadanand, Bal Mukund and Satyanand Munjal. *Standing (L-R)*: Jagdish Raheja (husband of sister Santosh) Brijmohan Lall and Om Prakash. Only four of the brothers went on to build the Hero Group.

The Hero Honda technical collaboration agreement being signed. Besides the Munjals, Koji Wanaka can be seen standing behind my father. Also in the frame on the extreme left is S.K. Mehta, who joined Hero straight out of college, retired as the legal head and went on to be one of the leaders of the foundation that runs BCM Schools.

My parents and three generations of their family at a picnic in the 1980s. These family get-togethers took place at regular intervals.

While Hero Honda has been c most celebrated collaborati Munjal Showa, an ancillary jo venture between the Munjals a Showa Corporation for maki shock absorbers, became o of the largest in its segme worldwide. Here, my fath with my uncles Satyanand a Om Prakash are seen at t inauguration of the venture.

Hero Cycles signed a joint ventu with National Panasonic to set Gujarat Cycles to manufacture a export high-end bicycles at t turn of the millennium. Here, r father and uncle follow the Indi tradition of exchanging swe to celebrate the milestone. T project never quite took off due a change in the partner's strate and the company only recover from the crisis on acquiri Gujarat government's stake a converting the venture into Mur Auto Industries, now a success auto-component maker.

Uncle Satyanand was passiona about the Arya Samaj, the Hin social reform movement th originated in the 19th centu Before work every day, he spe some hours doing Samaj wo Here, he is seen addressing t sect leaders.

6

Hero Powers Through

Ludhiana in the mid-1980s was a hub of wealth creation, but was still a relatively small town. Everybody who was anybody knew each other. Several of Punjab's bureaucrats counted themselves among our family's friends and would drop in every now and then. Among them was K.R. Lakhanpal, who was posted as deputy commissioner of the district from 1983–87.

He walked into my office one day and I could see from his expression that this wasn't a strictly social visit. It was a challenging time for the state bureaucracy, with Punjab in the grip of militancy. In 1984, India had suffered horrors that evoked painful memories from the past. Even as we celebrated the first Indian in space, preparations were secretly underway to send the army into the Golden Temple in Amritsar.

In the first week of June, ensconced in Pahalgam in Jammu and Kashmir on our annual family holiday, we watched in disbelief as Operation Blue Star unfolded on the TV screen. The army launched a frontal attack on the armed insurgents sheltering in the Golden Temple complex, over three days. The country had barely recovered from the shock when, on October 31, Prime Minister Indira Gandhi was assassinated by her Sikh bodyguards and in the next few hours, the unimaginable happened – mobs went wild and claimed the lives of thousands of Sikhs, mostly in Delhi.

For the senior Munjals, the Delhi riots of 1984 evoked painful memories of Partition. It was obvious to my father and my uncles that Punjab was heading for an unprecedented level of unrest, yet they refused to consider leaving. To their dismay, this meant having to accept security cover around the clock. The senior superintendent of police of Ludhiana got in touch with us, and suggested that security personnel be assigned for our protection which we refused.

Mr Lakhanpal wouldn't take no for an answer. Admittedly, from his perspective, he had good reason as Ludhiana had witnessed multiple instances of kidnappings, murders and threats of extortion in recent months. He had come to my office to inform me and to convey to the rest of the family that we really had no choice in the matter. He pointed out that if a mishap occurred involving any member of the family, it would be his neck on the chopping block. To our intense discomfort, he assigned a force to protect us – at our homes and factories and even to accompany us when we travelled. As soon as we could, we sent them back (many of our friends didn't, they quite enjoyed having an entourage that spelt 'VIP').

All through those turbulent years of militancy in the state of Punjab, neither Hero Cycles nor any of our manufacturing plants ever shut down, except on the day the army stormed Harmandir Sahib inside the Golden Temple at Amritsar. A curfew was declared for a few days, but our workers decided to stay in the factory premises and continue production, a testimony to their extraordinary level of commitment to the company. Food service and bedding had been arranged for the workers who were to stay in the plant, but soon work came to a halt. Our just-in-time (JIT) inventory management system ensured we had never had an inventory, so there were no godowns! The finished products were stacked in the corridors and wherever space was available. In any case, we soon ran out of components. So, for the first time, we had to stop production.

Sporadic violence apart, life in Punjab was by and large normal during the day, far from the public impression of bombs going off on a daily basis and gun-toting terrorists roaming around freely in search of hapless outsiders. The fear psychosis was such that you couldn't get anyone to come and visit Punjab, for love or money. When one of our generators broke down, we needed an insurance surveyor to come across from Delhi and assess our claim, but the gentleman kept making excuses. I had to literally buy him a ticket on a Vayudoot flight to Ludhiana and shame him into making the trip.

Sikh militancy, Operation Blue Star and its aftermath occurred at a very inopportune time for Hero. The joint venture agreement with Honda had been signed in 1984, and we had to get the venture off the ground as quickly as possible. My father did not have the slightest intention of deferring the launch of Hero Honda, come what may.

Funding was the first milestone we had to cross. Both promoters (Honda and us) pushed in their share of the equity capital of ₹6.2 crore one full year before the public issue. In fact, this was one of the reasons why confidence and faith in the promoters and the joint venture company was strong even before the factory was set up; the Hero Honda public issue, which took place in the wake of Indira Gandhi's assassination and the riots in Delhi, was oversubscribed by close to eleven times.

Our second milestone was to identify a suitable location for the proposed Hero Honda factory. Ludhiana was a comfort zone for the Munjals, but it did not have an international airport. Given that the Japanese would be advising Hero Honda's day-to-day operations and its officials would be constantly travelling to India, it was obviously not a desirable location. Honda was expected to send some forty engineers to help set up the factory, so it would have to be situated near a large city, with all amenities. Ludhiana also didn't fit the bill as it lacked an established set of automotive component manufacturers.

On the other hand, government policy demanded that new facilities be located in underdeveloped areas. To satisfy both requirements – those of Honda and the government – my father decided on Dharuhera in Haryana, which falls within what is now known as the National Capital Region (NCR). Its proximity to Delhi satisfied the Japanese and the Government of India's Industrial Policy deemed that the area was underdeveloped. The land was purchased and construction commenced.

Ramanji and Pawan were packed off to Delhi in 1984 and parked in the Hero guest house in East of Kailash in south Delhi, and expected to put their technical skills too experience to good use. Like all of us in the second generation, they too rigorously interned at a family firm, with our uncles or older cousins, serving as understudies.

These internships were not a cursory exposure to boardrooms; many of us had the opportunity to learn the nuts and bolts of the business from the ground up, leaving our egos outside the factory premises. We didn't just answer to our uncles, but to whoever was assigned to tutor us.

I don't know how many others did, but Suman and I had the good fortune to work with the inimitable Bhagatji, Hero's chief cashier. This gentleman epitomized the exceptional people who helped the Munjal brothers build Hero Cycles and the Hero Group. He was among the company's earliest employees, having joined as an accountant. His integrity was legendary. I observed that he always carried two sets of notebooks and two pens; when I asked him to explain why, he gave me an astonishing reply; he had bought one pen and notebook for personal use, and for official use, he used the company's stationary!

Eventually, when each of us had garnered adequate hands-on operational experience and proved ourselves, we were given a business to run or a division to set up. Ramanji had interned at Highway Cycles and then ran Highway Cycles, Pawan was with Majestic Auto, Yogesh at Rockman and so on. I was rotated between Hero Cycles, Rockman, Majestic Auto and Highway Cycles; thereafter, I got to set up Hero Fibres Ltd, our multi-fibre yarn spinning mill in Malerkotla, Punjab.

* *

My brothers relocated to Delhi to handle the joint venture, which, by then, had become a hot topic of discussion in the industry.

My father didn't turn a hair. The tie up with Honda was supposed to be Hero's launch pad into the big business world. Insofar as the Indian market was concerned, my father's vision was clear: Hero had always been a 'people's brand' and Hero Honda would be, too. He wanted his motorcycles to be accessible to the middle class segment. Hero's success lay in the reliability and competitive pricing of its products, as well as market penetration. The same formula, when applied to motorcycles, would redefine transportation in India. As it happened, Hero did that and more.

Digressing a bit, it must be mentioned here that Hero was in parallel negotiations with the Showa Corporation, a subsidiary of Honda, for a technical and financial collaboration for the manufacture of shock absorbers. Getting the go-ahead for the project was by no means simple.

A rival company was also keen on collaborating with Showa and did everything possible to stymie the deal with Hero. Finally, after a year of getting the bureaucratic run-around, the chairman of Showa told the *Economic Times* that if the company came to India, it would only be in collaboration with the Munjals. It was front-page news. The blunt, no-nonsense statement shook the government and the clearances came soon after. In 1985, Showa joined hands with us to manufacture shock absorbers and struts for two-wheelers and four-wheelers and, in time,

Munjal Showa eventually became amongst the largest manufacturers of two-wheeler shock absorbers in the world.

Coming back to the motorcycle story, my father's big coup was in getting the four-stroke engine technology. It was fuel-efficient and environment-friendly, but more expensive and far trickier to manufacture and assemble. This kind of motorcycle had not been manufactured or assembled in India before, so all the workers had to be trained.

The scale of my father's ambition must be emphasized here; he was looking to create a whole new market. In 1984–85, scooters dominated the two-wheeler market. Until then, clunky motorcycles were the norm, although Rajdoot's 'Bobby' bike, with its small frame and 75 cc engine, enjoyed a brief popularity after it featured in Raj Kapoor's 1973 cult film with the same name.

The insistence on affordability, durability and quality reflected a deep understanding of the Indian consumer. Hero's customer was aspirational yet frugal, ready and willing to move from bicycles and scooters to fuel-efficient motorcycles. The first to enter the market was TVS, with the Ind-Suzuki in 1984. In 1985, Escorts entered into a collaboration with Yamaha to make the Rx 100 and the 350 cc Yamaha Rajdoot. Bajaj was a late starter in the motorcycle segment and inked a deal with Kawasaki only in 1989.

The sheer genius of my father's insistence on fuel economy – 60 to 100 per cent better than the motorcycles of the 70s – became obvious at this point. The first Hero Honda motorcycle, the CD 100 was introduced to the Indian public with the unforgettable 1984 campaign by ad agency Ulka (now, FCB Ulka) based on the tag line: 'Fill it, Shut it, Forget it'.

The landscape of India would never be the same again. The scooter's dominance of Indian roads was over. As was Bajaj Auto's monopoly. The sleek-bodied Hero Honda stormed onto the scene and overtook every other two-wheeler on the road.There were many reasons for the success of Hero Honda, but creating a whole new market segment in the India of the 1980s and early 1990s was perhaps the most telling; while Suzuki, Yamaha, Kawasaki, Bajaj and TVS focused on urban youth as their primary customers for motorcycles, Hero Honda focused on the commuter.

* *

The Hero Honda CD 100 was a new-generation motorcycle that set industry yardsticks not just for fuel economy but for low emission, which made it the 'greenest' motorcycle on the roads at the time. It was the only four-stroke motorcycle in the 100 cc category. The other Japanese firms had supplied two-stroke engine technology to their Indian partners. Unlike the two-stroke engines, where carbon deposits collected on piston rings, spark plugs and silencers, the four-stroke engines caused much less pollution.

Since four-stroke engines were fundamentally more expensive to make, the CD 100 was priced a shade higher than competing products; however, the motorcycle more than compensated with higher fuel economy and lower maintenance costs, because it had the advantage of better engineered components and superior quality of service. This brought down the overall cost of ownership of a Hero Honda motorcycle, which was a significant plus for the Indian commuter.

My father, in an interview to *India Today* magazine in September 2001, succinctly conveyed his philosophy, 'The choice of a four-stroke motorcycle in the 1980s may sound providential, but we knew that buying a product is one thing and running it for a long time quite another. That is why we wanted the running cost of our vehicle to be low.'

This message, of paying slightly more upfront but far less over a period of time, was cleverly and effectively conveyed through TV and print campaigns, and it worked very well with the price-conscious emerging middle-class Indian of the 1980s. This new consumer was keen to migrate from cycles and mopeds, but couldn't quite afford a car, or even a motorcycle or a scooter with lower fuel efficiency and higher maintenance costs. My father took great pride in the durability of Hero

Honda motorcycles, and was delighted each time he heard that twenty and twenty-five-year-old CD-100s were still plying on the roads!

In its very first year, the CD 100 sold 40,000 units. In 1996-97, Hero Honda sold 2.7 lakh motorcycles while Bajaj sold 12.3 lakh. In 1995, Hero Honda launched Splendor, which went on to become the world's largest selling motorcycle in the years that followed. By 2001, Hero Honda had overtaken Bajaj in India. In the same year, Hero Honda became the world's number one two wheeler company in terms of unit volume sales in a calendar year.

My father's gamble had paid off, but higher sales did not necessarily mean profitability, as we soon discovered. In fact, for my father, who always wanted to balance profitability and market share, this was a matter of deep concern.

Just before the launch of the first Hero Honda bike in April 1985, a retail price of just over ₹10,000 was finalized. My father put his foot down; he wanted a four-figure price. Amit recalled, 'I went back to the Japanese and there was a lot of anguish and going back and forth. Still, Chairman Saab wouldn't budge. The first bike was finally launched with a four figure tag of ₹9990.' A year later, rising material costs and high taxes forced the company to raise prices to over ₹13,000.

Even after Hero Honda became the world's single largest two-wheeler company, 'Chairman Saab' would continue to be wary of price increases. He would call up dealers personally to assess the impact of a price hike. At one time, he made twenty-five to thirty calls across the country, almost a quarter of the total dealership strength at that point in time. Amit gently pointed out that it was the marketing department's job to interact with dealers. My father said it was not a question of responsibility. A personal call from the Chairman would make the dealer feel special and encourage him to make a bigger effort.

My father and uncle Om Prakash pioneered the concept of organized dealership networks where the company actually treated the sales channel as part of the family ecosystem. Hero Honda's dealership network became an entry barrier for our competition. The Munjal brothers knew the names of all the dealers and genuinely believed that in order to secure the company's personal bond with the dealer, their profitability had to be maintained at all costs.

My father made it a point to try and inculcate values for growth in Hero's dealers. He told them that they should invest for the future; of the income from the dealership, one-third should be invested in the business, one-third kept aside for growth and one-third spent on themselves. This may sound a tad paternalistic, but it gave the dealers a sense of comfort. The tradition of a Munjal family member being present at the dealers' family occasions was maintained and if the dealer happened to find himself financially stressed, a loan would be sanctioned every now and then to support them through difficult times.

As Ashok Taneja of Shriram Pistons once observed: 'You can talk to anyone who has been associated with respected Brijmohanji – an employee, a supplier or a dealer – and he will tell you a story of how he stretched himself to help others, in facilitating a bank loan, or in getting him a technology partner, or simply encouraging him to persevere in difficult circumstances.'

It cut both ways, of course. If a dealer's performance dipped, he would get a call from the head of sales. God forbid a dealer turned out to be a bad apple with unscrupulous practices; he would be sacked forthwith, yet if he was basically a sound chap going through hard times, Hero would support him until he was back on his feet. Until they became septugenarians, my father and uncle Om Prakash would travel extensively across the country, visiting dealerships and sussing out the competition. They would listen to complaints and problems and advise them on how to interact with customers: with humility, warmth and grace.

* *

The bulk of Hero Cycle dealers were ready to come on board and invest in new dealerships after Hero Honda was born, a testimony to their faith in the Munjal family elders. They were typically young, drawn from the next generation of the Hero dealers and eager to partner in the new venture, and equally important, willing to make the capital-intensive transition from *dukaan* (shop) to showroom.

My father played a key role in visualizing the showrooms, along with Ramanji. Clear criteria were fixed for training, signage, space, service quality and the investments that each dealer had to make. There were no compromises on this front and a Hero Honda dealer typically made higher investments in showrooms and workshops, as compared to those of competing brands like TVS Suzuki, Escorts Yamaha, Bajaj Kawasaki and Kinetic Honda. For instance, while their showrooms were 500 sq. feet, ours were 1,600 sq. feet. If a service centre was attached to the dealership, an additional 1,500 sq. feet were required.

The significantly higher investments in the workshops relative to the competition initially caused a lot of consternation amongst the dealers. They were worried that the higher investments would not be recouped, if the flow of business was similar to that of their competitors. In retrospect, they needn't have worried. First, revenues from the workshops overtook those from the showrooms; also, owners of competitor bikes began making a beeline for the workshops, as word spread in the market about the Hero Honda customer experience!

In that sense, Hero Honda was ahead of its time. The company understood that the market was shifting from a seller's to a buyer's market and tried to stay one step ahead of all marketing developments, while maintaining high quality standards. It kept the customer at the centre of all its strategies and more than 150 authorized service centres were set up within the first decade.

From 1985 to 1991, once every three weeks, my father would visit Delhi from Ludhiana and summon the entire marketing staff to the conference room. He would then deliver a masterclass on maintaining relationships with the Hero dealers: how to address the dealer, how to dress, what kind of courtesies one could accept from dealers, the importance of punctuality when visiting the dealership and so on. His thumb rule: if you have something nice to say to the dealer, convey it in writing so they could hold on to the message and even share it with others; harsh comments should be strictly verbal!

Recalling those times, Amit Chaturvedi said: 'We would all troop into the conference room. Chairman Saab would speak extempore. No agenda. No speaking points. He would just talk.' Many members of the staff would wait in anticipation for these sessions, in the expectation of receiving some nuggets they could hold on to and put into practice later.

Rahul Bajaj, the legendary chairman of Bajaj Auto, Hero Honda's fiercest competitor for many years, referred to my father as his guru. He attributed Hero Honda's success to my father's inter-personal relationships with his employees, vendors and distributors: 'I believe he treated them as members of his family, in a manner that none of us can do.' The entire enterprise, in fact, was built on the relationships that my father and uncles had created and nurtured.

* *

Yogesh once told me that the meetings and negotiations with the Japanese had taught him the importance of having fixed, rather than approximate, targets. The word 'estimate' did not figure in the Japanese business lexicon. 'I started thinking like them (the Japanese). In the course of the meetings I attended in Japan with Chachaji (Brijmohan), I realized that to succeed, you must think like your business partners also and understand their viewpoint. The very fact that we refrained from imposing only our personal or traditional outlook (on the JV) enabled us to work successfully with them for twenty-seven years.'

Working with the Japanese was by no means easy. Certainly, their companies were lauded for best practices, such as Total Quality Management (TQM) systems, Kanban and several others. Assimilating technology and processes was relatively simple; the big challenge lay in managing human capital. For example, the workers resistanted wearing the white clothes and gloves that Honda insisted on. Nor were they particularly enamoured by the Japanese-style early morning physical education sessions.

Skilled workers in India are independent-minded artisans who take pride in their craftsmanship. They regarded these little Japanese quirks as an imposition and were affronted. Ramanji, the company's leader and point man, understood and empathized with the workers, but had to tread a fine line between their expectations and those of Honda. By dint of persuasion and small compromises, he somehow found a middle path.

For instance, he decided not to create the post of a quality inspector, despite Honda's insistence. Ramanji suggested it might be better to trust and empower the employees instead. A monitor would make them feel belittled. Gradually, Hero Honda developed a bottom-up culture where workers, supervisors and managers were actively involved in problem-solving on the shop floor; in this way, a culture of collaboration evolved that was based on both the Indian and Japanese value systems.

Then, in the late 1980s, the environment for Japanese imports turned hostile. The Japanese yen rose sharply against the dollar. In 1984, when the Hero Honda project was being set up, the yen–rupee exchange rate stood at ¥2,100 to ₹100. It climbed inexorably from ¥960 to ₹100 in 1987, to ¥832 to ₹100 in 1988. Since many parts were imported from Japan, profitability was affected.

What made matters worse was that customs duty on components kept increasing in rupee terms. The rate remained the same, but the customs duty outgo in rupee terms kept increasing. Effectively, Hero Honda was making a loss on every motorcycle it was selling.

The heavy foreign exchange outgo prompted the Indian government to place restrictions on imports through tariff barriers. It became obvious that the CKD or SKD (semi-knocked down) approach, which involved local assembly rather than manufacture was not sustainable.

As production costs zoomed up, Hero Honda pushed some of the costs on to consumers, but not everything could be passed on. The price of the CD 100 was hiked thirteen times between 1985 and 1990; from ₹12,741 to ₹22,669, an increase of 78 per cent. By comparison, scooter prices rose by 40 per cent during this period. A 150 cc Bajaj scooter was then available for ₹11,000 as quoted in a business school case study. The downturn was reflected in the company's publicly listed share price. Quoted at ₹50 in 1985 at the time of listing, it plummeted to ₹15 in 1989. By 1990, the competition in the 100 cc segment had become intense, with the Bajaj Kawasaki, Rajdoot Yamaha and Ind-Suzuki all jostling for space.

Since the 1950s the government had promoted a phased manufacturing programme (PMP), encouraging indigenization through a variety of mechanisms, including import tariffs. Deploying this and other arguments, my father, ably assisted by Ramanji and Pawan, managed to convince the Japanese that critical components could be manufactured locally, instead of being imported. Indigenization, in fact, was one of the leitmotifs of setting up Hero Honda in the first place; but the efforts put in by my father and brothers ensured that we developed one of the fastest and most effective localization programmes in the auto industry.

The Japanese initially resisted the suggestion. They were sceptical whether the quality parameters could be consistently maintained. Also, the loss of revenue for Honda Trading (which imported components made by Honda's associates from across Asia) possibly played in the minds of our JV partner. Ramanji, who had had a ringside seat in the ancillarization process in Hero Cycles, along with Pawan at Majestic Auto, was confident that the manufacturing could be done locally at a lower cost, while maintaining the same quality. They argued that this would allow Hero Honda to price its products more competitively.

Amit Chaturvedi saw the push and pull negotiations unfold at close quarters. 'Whenever there was a pushback from Honda officials, Chairman Saab used his good equations with the government to send out a clear message to the Japanese, that localization could not be slowed; in fact, the government was keen that it should be speeded up, because of India's need to conserve foreign exchange," he recalled.

My father was persuasive and logical in his arguments, and made two pertinent points. First, a quick indigenization programme to make the company compliant with a major Government Policy would put the joint venture in the good books of policy makers; second, setting up a shining example of ancillarization would make Hero Honda's operations sustainable and lucrative as time went. Honda finally agreed to step up indigenization, and the two partners set up what turned out to be the world's largest auto indigenization programme.

Clearly, a world class and foolproof supply chain was required, so Ramanji decided to take a leaf from the Honda playbook. The auto major carried its ancilliaries along wherever it went and he was determined to do the same. He asked his friends, many of whom were in Ludhiana, to invest in component-manufacturing facilities around Dharuhera. All of them had been vendors for one or other of the Hero Group companies, had considerable experience of engineering and tool-making, but possessed very little domain knowledge of the specialized components required for motorcycles. They knew that getting into the comparatively less tested domain of motorcycles was a risk, but such was their conviction about the Munjals, that they agreed.

In a span of a few years, many vendors, mostly close friends of my elder brother Ramanji either expanded their production lines for Hero Honda or set up new operations, or relocated to the NCR, creating a wonderful ecosystem of collaboration and learning. They included Krishan Jajoo of Hema Auto, Arvind Kapur of Rico Auto Industries, Jatender Mehta of Omax Autos, Rakesh Dhingra and Sanjeev Mehta of Autofit, V.P. Bajaj of Bajaj Motors, Verinder Chhabra of Unitech, Deep Kapuria of Hi Tech Gears, Jayant Davar of Sandhar Group, Pravin Malhotra of Nipman Fasteners, Raj Bhatia of Bony Polymers, Atul Raheja of Lifelong India, Vipin Raheja of Napino India, Gopi Kothari of Kay Jay Forgings, Surinder Mahendru of Nicks Auto, Sanjeev Soni of Meenakshi Polymers, D K Jain of Lumax, and Nirmal Minda of Minda Auto.

The Gurgaon–Dharuhera component cluster created some of the best-known brands in auto parts. Rakesh Dhingra and Sanjeev Mehta's Autofit is India's largest manufacturer of two-wheeler seats. Jayant Davar's Sandhar Group has three subsidiaries and seven joint ventures, with thirty-five factories all over the world. Arvind Kapur's Rico Auto is now a global supplier of automotive components with fourteen manufacturing plants, 4,500 employees and a presence in four continents. Jatender Mehta's Omax Autos, which provides a wide gamut of tubular auto assemblies, today has nine facilities across India.

Today, they are big component firms, but the first phase of their journey was anything but easy. To begin with, a pilot production programme was initiated to test the indigenization capabilities of the vendors. Unfortunately, the first batch of a large number of locally produced components failed to pass quality tests.

Every so often Ramanji and my father would sit down with the vendors and discuss their problems, be it labour issues or government regulations. The collective brainstorming invariably led to positive outcomes.

Jatender Mehta of Omax Autos, one of the vendors who faced teething problems, recalls:

> There was plenty of handholding and all problems were solved together. I remember we were facing some quality and marketing issues in the initial days. Ramanji convinced the faculty at the Indian Institute of Management (IIM) Ahmedabad to design a special programme that would help us to upskill and develop capabilities. This was a completely unheard-of practice at ancillaries those days.
>
> When Chairman Saab was president of the Confederation of Engineering Industry (CEI; predecessor of CII), the TQM movement had started gaining popularity in the Indian industry for the first time and he ensured that all the key vendor units received exposure to TQM.

> Looking back, all the transitions of Hero Honda were smooth, because of this handholding process, and the value creation that took place on the shop floor through sustained problem solving was meaningful and successful. It was an exciting period, when we were exposed to concepts like 'why-why' analysis and root cause analysis. We also learnt to peel a problem, layer by layer, reaching its genesis. From introducing statistical tools to gemba kaizen (continuous improvement) to Business Process Re-engineering, whatever was done at Hero Honda was replicated on the vendor shop floors.
>
> Even as Hero Honda grew and the number of SKUs (stock keeping units) grew along with the number of models, we, as vendors, never felt overwhelmed. We were candid enough to list our challenges upfront and immediately. Hero Honda pitched in, even if it meant sending teams on deputation. We even had Japanese experts coming in and working with us.

Here, I must mention that in the first decade and a half, while we were in the process of setting up and consolidating our operations, we developed an excellent relationship with a number of Honda officials. They were of great help in the early years and helped us overcome a number of the teething challenges. Yuji Saito was the first joint managing director of Hero Honda, K Sugiyama was the first technical director, T Fujisaki was responsible for all Hero Honda matters in Japan, and later became joint MD. Then there was Shibata San who set up quality systems, Yanagida San who set up production planning systems, Suzuki San who played a key role in the production ramp up and engine development project, and Nagai San who helped set up the best in class after sales network.

Jatender Mehta recalls:

> By the early 1990s, the vendors managed to supply parts that satisfied the rigorous standards and high expectations of the Japanese. The supply chains were completely aligned, especially

through the 1990s. This was the period in which Pawan, who was the technical director at Hero Honda, used his deep understanding of technology to play a critical role.

We saw that in later years, many of the ancillary practices that Hero Honda institutionalized, were emulated by competitors such as Bajaj and TVS. In fact, many of us feel that Maruti, too, learned from our experience and tweaked their vendor practices.

The ability of many of these firms to scale up from small operations had a lot to do with my father's insistence on decoupling from the Ludhiana modus operandi. According to Amit Chaturvedi, 'Chairman Saab played a critical role in ensuring that when the company started, there was no interference from the cycle ecosystem or (infusion of) the Ludhiana culture in the motorcycle ecosystem. Keeping the larger family away from interfering in day-to-day business was one of Chairman Saab's biggest contributions to the success of not just the joint venture, but also the growth of many of the family businesses that came up along the Dharuhera–Gurgaon belt and in setting best in class governance practices.'

Uncle Om Prakash also eventually understood that selling a bicycle was not quite the same as selling a motorcycle and was smart enough to step back. While suggestions and strategic ideas from the larger family were always welcomed, the concept of professionalizing operations began to gain currency from this period.

Another challenge was finding common ground to overcome the cross-cultural divide. For instance, my father was a teetotaller who did not encourage drinking. This was a huge challenge while managing a joint venture with growing marketing and sales teams, as well as JV partners who were parked in India with large teams for months at a time. As Amit pointed out in amusement, 'The Japanese loved their drinks at meetings and conferences, as also in their leisure time!' A solution was clearly required.

Ramanji at first suggested that while the Japanese could be served out of courtesy, Hero staffers would be told to refrain from tippling. However, he soon realized the limitations of this plan, so a compromise was struck. When my father was around, nobody from Hero would drink! It was quite a hilarious affair. Scouts would be posted and whenever my father entered a venue, an alert would be sounded and glasses would quickly be switched.

I am certain my father knew what was going on behind his back but chose to turn a blind eye out of kindness. Amit recalled, 'I think Chairman Saab knew all the time that we drank in those days!'

* *

The group expanded all through the 1980s and 1990s. Yet Hero Honda did face its share of challenges. Shortly after the Hero Honda plant at Dharuhera was started, the company faced adversity by way of a strike in 1986. This was surprising, since the company's compensation and work environment has always been among the best in India.

Nevertheless, in our eagerness and desperation we even approached some of the local leaders for their help. Jatender and I went chasing a Haryana politician during an election rally from village to village, trying to get him to talk to relevant authorities and union leaders.

The Dharuhera strike in the early days showed the strength and resolve of the family and its ecosystem. The different units of the family, friends and business partners all came together and solved the many issues of the day, this was a practice that got institutionalized over the decades.

In fact, the beauty of the relationship lay in the fact that despite individual differences that may have cropped up from time to time amongst some of the members, the family always pulled together especially when it came to the larger interest of the family and the business.

My father made it a point to involve friends, family and employees in the business, by encouraging them to set up their own component units, thereby creating a 'Hero-first' supply chain. Munjal Showa (shock absorbers, 1985), Sunbeam Castings (aluminium die castings, 1987) and Munjal Castings (mufflers and spoke rims, 1981), were set up by uncle Satyanand's children Yogesh, Ashok and Sudhir.

Sunbeam Auto has grown beyond supplying to the family flagship and is a key supplier to India's top carmaker Maruti, in addition to being an international supplier of Ford, Continental and Bosch. Munjal Auto (formerly Gujarat Cycles) started out as an export-oriented unit to meet the needs of the international bicycle markets, now makes light engineering automotive products, including autorims, forgings and wheels, and supplies both the international and national markets.

My sister Geeta and her family set up AG Industries for (plastic-moulded components). The company now has seven facilities across four states.

Orders placed by Hero enabled these companies to negotiate better rates for raw material and improve their margins, a slice of which was passed on to Hero as preferential pricing resulting in a win-win situation all around. For instance, in 1998, we estimated that 65 per cent of outsourced components for Hero Honda came from our own companies. Of course, as mentioned earlier, the component units supplied to the entire industry.

The Hero Group also had adequate surpluses to fund diverse ventures. My father said they had money to invest because they believed in cost control and not in splurging to feed their vanity. Economies of scale and better technology naturally aided the process. As my uncle Om Prakash noted, there was a time when two and a half people produced one cycle, but by the 1990s, a single person could produce three cycles.

Hero Motors, helmed by my cousin Pankaj, in collaboration with Steyr Puch (owned by Daimler-Benz) of Austria, got off the ground in Ghaziabad that same year. My father said, 'Investments of ₹20–30 crore will not lead us anywhere. A big project requires the same amount of time, the same amount of knocking on doors, as a small one.' A new Hero Cycles plant, with the capacity to manufacture half a million bicycles, was set up in Sahibabad in Uttar Pradesh. Gujarat Cycles (later Munjal Auto Industries) was established in 1985 and in 1990, the Hero Cold Rolled steel unit came up in Ludhiana.

Suman, my elder brother, expanded the operations of Rockman Industries beyond auto chains and hubs in the first decade of the new millennium, setting up a unit in Haryana to make aluminium die-casting components and alloy wheels. Rockman now has eight plants with the addition of two new units in Gujarat and Andhra Pradesh. Members of the third generation are now working in next-generation manufacturing technologies such as carbon composites.

My father always took great pride in the fact that my daughter, Shefali, was one of the first members of the third generation to take the responsibility of running the IT services business at Hero Corporate Service. He would have been equally proud of her if he had learnt that the family insurance distribution business – which she took over in 2006 – has now become the largest business for insurance distribution in the country.

Most of these expansions have come through internal accruals, and a remarkable aspect of Hero firms over the years has been their relatively debt-free balance sheets. There were many reasons for this, including the ability to manage inventories and generate free cash flows, but it is important to appreciate the cost savings that stemmed from the impulse to be self-sufficient and self-reliant. Here, my father took the lead on many occasions.

Rakesh Vasisht, who joined Hero Honda in 2000, worked with my father as his executive assistant for many years and had a ringside view of his operating style. Rakesh recalls my father as being absolutely hands-on. Every day, he would come into work and look at four things: receivables, inventory levels in the premises, level of dispatch to dealers and customer complaints. He tracked these with a hawk's eye and during the day, he asked Mrs Vijaya Chaudhry, who managed the phone systems on his floor, to put him through to one dealer per zone. In those days, there were four zones in all. That was his way of getting his ear to the ground, without the corporate bureaucracy coming in the way!

Rakesh observed: 'When it came to planning and execution, Chairman Saab had this great ability to detach himself and take a helicopter view when needed, and become granular when necessary. For example, in the early days when I had joined, he used to scrutinize and approve all large ticket expenses. If new equipment was required, he planned a factory visit and went right to the spot where the machine was required; he would call all the involved departments, and conduct a typical time and motion study, with questions on layout, power supply, environmental discharge and material flows. On almost every occasion, he looked to optimize costs, increase efficiency and save time.

'He invariably had questions on procurement; whether it was possible to source parts of the machine from India, instead of importing it. At times, from a fully imported machine, we evolved to a situation where the heart of the machine was imported, while the non-essential parts were locally made. His logic was simple: Hero Honda should not compromise on quality, but if it was possible to bring down overall capital cost, it should be done.'

It is our assessment that this level of execution helped cut costs drastically, often by a factor of 30 to 50 per cent.

7

Losing a Beloved

'We are not supposed to outlive our children,' says Nina, a character in *An Unfinished Life*. I don't think my father ever saw that film, with Robert Redford playing the bereaved dad, but he would have empathized with the wealth of pain behind that line of dialogue. Children are not meant to pre-decease their parents; losing a child is a perversion of the natural order of things. However, it happens and, tragically, my parents were among the those who suffered such an irreparable loss.

On the evening of 18 June 1991, Ramanji went to the gym. A couple of hours later, he was no more. That's all we knew. The why and how and when of it occurred to us much later, after we had begun to emerge from near catatonic shock. Grief engulfed the entire Munjal family and our universe. Ramanji had been a son, brother, husband, father, nephew, cousin and a wonderful friend, so everyone had lost a part of their lives. Never was the collective strength of the family more needed than on that hot June day in 1991.

Ramanji had left his office at Delhi's Vikram Hotel and headed to his gym in Greater Kailash II for his workout. He was on a fitness kick and in fairly good shape; an executive health check-up a few weeks earlier had given him a clean bill of health. Our cousin Jatender, who was his closest buddy, was with him. They hit the machines; Ramanji was on the treadmill, when he suddenly stopped and sat down, saying he felt uncomfortable. He told Jatender to carry on with his workout, while he rested. After a bit, he said it seemed like his heart was giving out.

He left the gym, got into his car and told Punditji, his driver, to take him to the Escorts Heart Institute as fast as possible. The hospital was around five kilometers away. Midway, he told Punditji the agony was 'too extreme' and he might not make it, so they had best stop at the National Heart Institute, which was en route. He was fully conscious when he was carried into the Emergency ICU and was even able to speak to the staff, but in a matter of minutes, he had succumbed to a massive cardiac arrest. Two weeks short of his forty-second birthday, he was gone.

All of us remember where we were, when this traumatic event took place. My father happened to be in Delhi for a wedding. Mr Rai, who was sitting with him at the time, told me that when the phone call came, my father could not comprehend what had happened.

Denial is the first of the classic five stages of grief and that's how it was with him. His spiritual moorings enabled him to skip over the intervening stages of anger and bargaining, but he moved into the fourth phase: depression. He stayed over at Ramanji's home in Greater Kailash Part I, with Amit in attendance. All through the night, he kept saying he must have done something very wrong in the past, that's why his son had been taken from him. He even speculated whether

Ramanji's decision to move into a new home was a stroke of bad luck. Within a short time though, both my parents had delved into their deep spiritual reserves and reached the final phase, of acceptance and reconciliation.

I was in Ludhiana when we received the call, back from one of my frequent trips to Delhi and Sanawar, where my daughter was studying. Suman, Renuka Bhabhi ('bhabhi' is a term of respect for a sister-in-law) and I hastily boarded the overnight train to Delhi and arrived well in time for the funeral. At the Lodhi Road Crematorium that day, my siblings and I found our father quite composed. Sitting under a tree, at some distance from the pyre, he spoke about the '*bhog*' (prayer ceremony) in Ludhiana: where should it be held, how many people were likely to attend and so on.

He spoke of Renu, my late brother's widow, and how important it was that she did not get too much time or space to grieve and should emerge from this dark phase of her life with a sense of dignity and self-worth.

My father regained a measure of resilience and sublimated his grief in planning for the future, from the immediate funerary rituals to long-term plans for the company. His immediate concern was Renu, whom Ramanji had married in 1974, and their three children, fifteen-year-old Rahul, twelve-year-old Radhika, and eight-year-old Abhimanyu, who would need all the emotional and moral support the family could provide. He planned to coax his daughter-in-law to accompany him to the office every day and sit with him through the day (a practice which continued right up to his own demise in 2015).

My father followed through with these plans. He had a desk installed for Renu right next to his own in the office and involved her in the financial services arm of the group, Hero Honda Finlease (now Hero FinCorp). He helped her set up a foundation in Raman's memory and ensured that she stayed actively involved in its projects. Today, the Raman Kant Munjal Foundation runs multiple education and skill initiatives, and has played a key role in mainstreaming and developing a backward region of Haryana. My father also mentored her three young children and made sure they did not suffer because of their father's absence. Both Rahul and Abhimanyu went on to independently manage sizeable businesses.

The tragedy would have broken a lesser mortal, but my father picked up the pieces and moved on. He knew the pain of loss would never go away, but life had to go on. After the tragedy, my parents spiritual inclinations became more pronounced. Havans had been a daily feature in our homes ever since I could remember, as were the *sadhus* who visited our homes, factories and offices. Hereafter, the number and frequency of these visits and prayer meetings increased.

* *

Ramanji left behind a void that was difficult to fill. He was unusual, in the sheer quantum and range of activities he had packed into his forty-two years. He was family oriented, like our father. So much so that he had quit his engineering course at the Manipal Institute of Technology, because he wanted to be closer to home. He'd tried to settle down at Manipal, even starting a Punjab Club and lobbying to introduce north Indian cuisine in the mess, but missed home far too much. The family elders consented to his joining the Thapar Institute of Engineering and Technology in Patiala, a couple of hours' drive from Ludhiana. Even then, his tendency to slip off to Chandigarh to visit Jatender and their friends, left him lamentably short of attendance.

Like all the Munjal sons, he interned at family-owned facilities. My mother recalls that he wanted to take charge of Highway Cycles when it was launched in 1971, at the grand old age of twenty-two! Highway Cycles was set up after my father and uncles had had enough of the inferior quality free wheels that were supplied by local vendors.

Obviously, Ramanji had to wait but he gradually earned his stripes and became the centrepoint of Hero Honda. He was spontaneous and jocular and enjoyed being at the centre of activity. I remember how, when the first batch of motorcycles rolled out of the Hero Honda factory, he jumped up and joined the bhangra (a traditional dance of the Indian subcontinent, originating in Punjab) troupe that had been called in for a performance.

As mentioned earlier, many of the vendors who had set up ancillaries at Dharuhera were his friends. While most businessmen avoided appointing family members or friends as vendors, for fear that it would lead to a conflict of interest, my father always said that the practice offered a dual advantage. It not only resulted in closer coordination with suppliers, but ensured regular supply, quality control, lower costs, and a higher commitment, thus creating better chances of success.

Our Japanese partners were naturally concerned. Within the industry, it was widely known that the joint venture was run by Hero. Ramanji was the fulcrum, tasked with overseeing a partnership between two diverse organizations with dramatically different cultures and building a business in a market where fresh competition was emerging by the day. Pawan had been at his elbow and the two had complemented each other. Temperamentally, Ramanji and Pawan were poles apart. Ramanji was effusive and social, Pawan reticent and private; Ramanji was a big-picture guy, Pawan was detail-oriented, and focused more on the plants, and the manufacturing.

He was not yet prepared to step into Raman's shoes and, more to the point, the Japanese would have been equally reluctant. Nor did we want a Japanese leading the company, because they wouldn't have understood the Indian ethos and the cultural milieu of that era. My father decided to move from Ludhiana to Delhi and take charge of the company as chairman and managing director. So the company was stabilized right away while business went back to normal and continued to grow.

Ramanji's place on the board of Hero Honda was filled by uncle Satyanand. My father continued as CMD (Chairman and Managing Director), with uncle Om Prakash and Pawan serving as directors. In Ludhiana, there was something of a vacuum, because my father's focus on Hero Honda meant that he had to pull back from his role in the rest of the group. He had little option; the entire industry was going through a challenging phase and was yet to stabilize in terms of both growth and profitability. Most of the day-to-day decisions were increasingly taken by uncle Om Prakash as he began to cover areas that were earlier handled by my father. My father and uncle, nevertheless, continued to remain closely and frequently in touch on the phone.

8

Becoming the Two-Wheeler Leader

By the early 1990s, I was already working with my father in managing the corporate office for the Hero Group and with my father taking on a more active role at Hero Honda, I had to take full charge as the strategic planner and public face of the group. As my father drastically reduced his interaction with external stakeholders, I had to step up my engagement, especially with policymakers and decision-takers in government.

Fortunately, I always had an interest in this role and considerable experience in collective action for problem-solving and establishing best practices. I became president of the Malerkotla Industries Association in my late twenties and also stepped into my father's shoes in the Ludhiana Management Association (LMA). He was LMA president for two terms, then after a gap, I served for another two terms.

All through the next few decades, my father would encourage my involvement in policymaking. Perhaps he felt it was a way of serving the industry, country and society beyond the realm of the company.

While my father started a culture of maintaining a neutral stance towards politics, the group developed a policy for working with government or regulatory bodies to generate good ideas and thoughts by either being members on different committees, or by actively providing quality inputs for policy and other decision-making, including implementation ideas.

Due to his neutral stand and friendly nature, and knowing fully that whenever he made a recommendation it would be for the good of the industry, economy and country, and never for a specific benefit for our own firms, my father was accepted as a genuine friend by people across the political spectrum including individuals like Arun Jaitley, Lal Krishna Advani, Atal Behari Vajpayee and Venkaiah Naidu. He also interacted closely with Rajiv Gandhi, Dr Manmohan Singh, Kamal Nath, Bhupinder Hooda, Anand Sharma, and many others.

Taking the cue from my father, I found myself serving on numerous panels, including the Narsimhan Committee (on banking reform), the Kelkar committee (on taxation reform) and the Prime Minister's Council on Trade and Industry. Once, when I turned down a request to serve on the board of the Life Insurance Corporation (LIC), the powers that be reached out to my father, who gently nudged me to at least consider taking on the job. Needless to say, I did.

My father had been CII president in 1988–89. It was a critical role at that point in time, because the Indian economy was poised to open up. Numerous reform programmes which were implemented in 1991 were of course conceived during the 1985–89 period. There was a growing view that India's strengths should be leveraged in different ways; for example, my father recalled Prime Minister Rajiv Gandhi telling CII that it was time Indian businesses thought global and to that end, insisted it send a team to the World Economic Forum. He also believed that the Indian expertise in mathematics could put us on the global map in computer technology.

Thanks to CII and my father's encouragement, I had a ringside seat to the groundwork for India's transformation into a high-quality global economy. I recall economists and thinkers like Rakesh Mohan, Jairam Ramesh, Montek Singh Ahluwalia and Sam Pitroda coming to CII in the late 1980s and ideating with Tarun Das, the CII director general. To me, it sounded like the scripting of a second freedom movement. The Licence Raj was gradually moving towards relaxation, but had not been lifted. Indeed, under Finance Minister V.P. Singh in the latter half of the 1980s, certain industrialists were subjected to a 'raid raj'.

* *

While the difficulties being faced by the economy were well known, the currency crisis of 1991 came as a shock.

In January 1991, as India struggled to finance its essential imports, especially oil and fertilizers, and to repay official debt, senior officials managing the economy in the Chandra Shekhar government reached out to influential members of the global financial system. It was in difficult circumstances that they did so: poor economic management in the preceding years had led to a rapidly deteriorating environment, exacerbated by the Gulf War, which triggered a spike in oil prices.

Amidst the mounting economic pressures, the Chandra Shekhar government fell in February 1991, and was reduced to a caretaker status. By mid-March, global credit-rating agencies had placed India on the watch list and, by April, had downgraded the country's sovereign rating from investment grade to a notch lower, making it virtually impossible to raise even short-term funds.

Without a full budget and a firm commitment to reforms, multilateral institutions such as the International Monetary Fund

(IMF) and the World Bank, the major lenders at the time, discontinued their funding. Bilateral assistance from other countries also wasn't forthcoming, with very few exceptions. Faced with a severe liquidity crisis and the very real prospect of defaulting on sovereign payments, time was running out. Senior government officials moved a proposal to pledge India's gold reserves.

In the middle of the election campaign of 1991, marred by the assassination of Rajiv Gandhi in Sriperumbudur on May 21, Finance Minister Yashwant Sinha, who was in Patna at the time, approved the proposal to mortgage the gold. The government decided on what appeared to be a politically smart course of action: to send the gold out a few days after polling, with consignments being airlifted between May 21 and 31.

The Swiss group, UBS Group AG, had bought the gold, enabling India to raise $200 million. Ensuring secrecy was a challenge. The consignments were tested to ensure that they met the requisite standards and were shipped off on a chartered plane. The decision to pledge gold was severely criticized when it later became public.

The new government which came to power in June 1991, headed by P.V. Narasimha Rao and with Manmohan Singh as finance minister, was confronted with the task of swiftly raising resources, given the country's precarious balance of payments. Forex reserves were barely adequate to cover even three weeks of imports.

Between 4–18 July 1991, the RBI pledged 46.91 tonnes of gold with the Bank of England and the Bank of Japan to raise $400 million. As the economic situation improved, the government repurchased the gold before December that year and transferred it to the RBI. But this time around, the political fallout was extensive; after *Indian Express* broke the story of gold being pledged, Manmohan Singh was compelled on explain in Parliament that it was a painful necessity.

Sweeping reforms were another painful necessity, and the Congress government initiated an ambitious programme of deregulation that included large-scale delicensing of industry, permitting foreign direct investment in multiple sectors, abolition of FERA, etc. In July 1991, a sharp devaluation of the rupee by ₹17 came into force.

The foreign exchange crisis in early 1991 was the final trigger, but we knew that liberalization was the result of a deliberate and conscious set of moves. What is less well known, is the fact that a lot of the early groundwork had already been done – India had been contemplating economic reforms for several years. It wasn't as if we suddenly woke up one day and changed everything because the IMF told us to. Yet the big benefit of the crisis was that the reforms were not done piecemeal, but in one sweeping move.

It was this preparatory effort that helped Narasimha Rao and Manmohan Singh implement radical changes in a reasonably short period, despite the intense opposition. In fact, the government faced a continual barrage of accusations – that it had bowed to pressure from the IMF and the World Bank, exposed the country to renewed imperialism and set it on the path of economic slavery to the West. The outcome, of course, was entirely different and belied the fears of the naysayers. The Indian economy moved into a higher gear and has continued to go from strength to strength. In fact, no large democracy, anywhere in the world, has grown as consistently over the last three decades as India has.

The challenges of poverty and agricultural distress are yet to be resolved, but positive changes and the potential for further changes, are there for all to see. There's little doubt that India will be amongst the three leading economies of the world, and will actively shape global geopolitics in the coming decades.

Having directly witnessed the stupendous turnaround of recent decades, I am confident that India has the wherewithal and ability to overcome the toughest of challenges, and will do so responsibly, with an eye on equitability, viability and sustainability.

As for the automotive sector, I can state with assurance that my family's ethos and work culture had an impact on the business, which in turn influenced the entire industry. The auto industry today is a pioneer of modern manufacturing and business practices and this has had a significant multiplier effect on the economy through the creation of high-quality jobs and the introduction of modern R&D and superior technology. The outcome has been a hyper-competitive market focused on customer service and efficiency; even more importantly, it has led to a business culture where competitors are able to sit across a table and discuss issues of common interest.

* *

For us, baby steps towards liberalization had begun in 1983, when joint ventures in the two-wheeler sector were allowed. Post-reforms, the group entered a period of consolidation and growth. In 1991, we set up Hero Honda Finlease to finance two-wheeler purchases; in 1993 came Hero Exports, which would go on to become India's largest exporter of bicycles, and Hero Financial Services.

The growth of consumerism in the 1990s matched the increase in purchasing power and along with the popularization of easy monthly instalments (EMIs), fuelled the motorcycle market. Plus, the public transport system was quite abysmal and bikes purchased in the 1980s now needed replacing; so both factors buoyed sales. We had stolen a march over the competition with our four-stroke technology and introduced the Sleek in 1989 and the souped-up CD 100 SS, aimed at the rural and mofussil market in 1991.

In fact, Hero Honda opened up the rural market. Motorcycles offered greater comfort than small-wheeled scooters on rural terrain. Post-sales service infrastructure was gradually built up and from a 4:1 ratio between the urban and rural markets in 1990, it would be practically even by the end of the decade.

However, production constraints were bogging down the motorcycle business. My father was acutely conscious of the need for technologically superior models and knew he couldn't go back to the market with the same old thing, year after year. Once the four-stroke engine monopoly came to an end, the customer would have to be offered something else. The Hero Honda Splendor was launched in 1994 against the backdrop of this thinking and proved to be a game-changer by the turn of the decade. Fortunately as well, by this time the worst of the economic crisis was over.

* *

By the early 1990s, the rupee-yen exchange rate had somewhat stabilized and 90 per cent indigenization had been achieved. It would improve to 95 per cent by 1996, a record for a Honda plant overseas and probably for any automotive plant in the world. The beneficial effects of indigenization kicked in only gradually since integration of vendors into supply chain took time and this led to production constraints. However, the share price moved up as imports came down and in terms of CKD value, whereas a bike had ¥65,000 worth of imported parts in 1985, the figure had dropped to ¥7,800 in 1994.

In 1994 – the year that my father was honoured with the prestigious Businessman of the Year award by business magazine *Business India* – Honda reaffirmed its partnership with Hero for the next ten years. Much of the credit for the durability of this partnership goes to my father.

He and Pawan would hold an informal meeting with the two Honda senior directors stationed at the company headquarters every month; decisions would be taken and implemented before the next meeting. As he would say: 'Even in the toughest stages of decision-making in our joint venture, there were no strains and crucial strategic issues were resolved in a very congenial approach.' (Pawan later revealed that he had a hard time negotiating with one particular representative of Honda.)

The uncertainty surrounding the JV agreement with Honda had an impact, leading to production constraints and inadequate number of models being introduced. The entry of other players with four-stroke variants, also took a toll and for a brief period, Bajaj Auto overtook

Hero Honda in terms of market share in 1995 and launched its KB 4S (four stroke) with the tongue-in-cheek tagline '*Kyon Hero*?'.

The technical collaboration extension agreement, led to a decisive turnaround, and Hero Honda initiated plans to expand its range of products and production capacity. Stricter emission norms from 1997 onwards ensured that our competitors had to withdraw their two-stroke motorcycles. This is where my father's absolute insistence during the launch to go in for the environment friendly four-stroke technology, instead of the relatively inexpensive two-stroke technology, proved to be a masterstroke. The Yamaha RX-l00 to RX-132, Bajaj KB 100 to KB125, and TVS-Shogun were off the roads, leaving the field relatively clear for Hero Honda.

Annual production at Dharuhera increased from 150,000 to 450,000 from 1994 to 1997, despite rising costs, thanks to my father's mantra – get the best out of men, material, and machines and to minimize waste. The cost of raw materials had gone up sharply in 1995, which was addressed by recycling scrap while production processes were streamlined to minimize interruptions and inventory management upgraded.

The dealer network increased in tandem with sales. Starting with 120 dealerships in 1985, it expanded to 375 by 1998, about half of whom were former Hero Group dealers. A year earlier, we had opened a second Hero Honda plant in Gurgaon to further scale up production, and it was inaugurated by Nobuhiko Kawamoto, the President of Honda Motors.

At around the same time, Hero Honda launched a new motorcycle, the Street, with great fanfare. On Honda's insistence, it was launched on Bajaj Auto's home turf, Pune! My father always said it wasn't a contest; the share of the two-wheeler pie didn't matter, as long as companies grew the market and made profits. Based on the Honda Dream, a worldwide hit, it signalled that all was well between Hero and Honda. The launch focused on rider comfort and was supported by a sharply increased ad-spend.

By 1997–98, Hero Honda Motors was back in pole position. Production figures climbed inexorably and passed the one-million mark in 2000–01. The Passion was launched in 2001 and the best-selling CD Dawn in 2003, cementing Hero Honda's leadership in two-wheelers.

* *

I mentioned earlier that from his experience at Hero Cycles, my father understood the needs of the aspirational Indian more than most. His hands-on interactions at Hero Honda also taught him that the motorcycle buyer and the motorcycle dealer of the new millennium were different from the cycle buyer of the 1970s; he or she wanted a good deal.

This is when my father and Pawan decided to turn both channel partners and customers into brand ambassadors, through win-win relationships, which in any case formed the core of my father's business philosophy.

In 2001, a pioneering initiative was launched: the Hero Passport Programme which was upgraded to the Good Life programme in 2004. As customer relationship management (CRM) schemes went, it was one of the most novel and successful of the era. Customers could accumulate points with every purchase of spares or accessories and every service at a Hero Honda dealership or service centre while referrals earned bonus points. Apart from discounts and freebies like tickets to events, the customer was eligible for a ₹1 lakh accident insurance cover. In 2004, Hero Honda partnered with the State Bank of India to introduce the first co-branded credit card in the two-wheeler industry.

There were incentive schemes for dealers as well. Pawan would take the top fifty dealers to Japan, where they visited the Honda factories, showrooms and service centres. This not only kept them motivated, but gave them a deeper understanding of the product they were selling and a fresh perspective on sales promotion, which induced dealers to invest in their businesses. Standout dealers who did well could avail of holidays in Europe with their wives. Hero Honda would pay half the cost of the holiday and help in organizing tour details, like hotel bookings, visas, foreign exchange and travellers cheques and so on. At the time, this was a huge incentive for dealers in small towns and peri-urban areas.

* *

The late 1990s and the early part of the new millennium saw hectic activity in India's automotive sector. Foreign investors began showing great interest in ramping up their Indian operations as the size of the market grew. Our family too began to explore options beyond its core portfolio of products.

Hero Motors tied up with Malaguti of Italy to create a large-wheeled scooter called the Winner. It also made a bid for Scooters India and explored a partnership with BMW for high-end motorcycles. Unfortunately, these ventures didn't reach fruition.

Meanwhile, Honda became more ambitious about its India footprint. The renewed 1994 JV agreement also allowed Hero to venture into the scooter market and Honda into motorcycles, but it was in 1999 that Honda set up its wholly owned subsidiary, to make motorcycles and scooters on its own in India. It decided to go with the Shriram group in the car segment (Honda Siel Cars Limited) and also partnered with them in the manufacture of portable generators.

Honda initially wanted to work with us as a JV partner, but made their intent of controlling the company very clear; this didn't suit us because we strongly believed that our successful JV model could easily be replicated across another product category.

My father was disappointed for a number of reasons. First, making a natural progression up the transportation value chain, from cycles to mopeds to motorcycles and scooters and, finally, to four wheelers, had been a long-cherished dream of his. For him, this journey symbolized the complete evolution of Hero. So when the deal with Honda didn't materialize, he didn't hide his disappointment, because he was convinced that the two partners would be able to pull it off again.

Second, my father was a little hurt that the Honda management was less accommodative in its stance. Those Japanese executives whom he'd dealt with in the previous decade were no longer around and the appetite for collaboration, negotiation and give and take wasn't as strong in the new leadership. I think my father was also a little upset that Honda was aggressively pursuing its own plans for motorcycles and scooters, even as the JV was going strong.

Yet the Hero Honda joint venture stayed par for the course and despite the rumblings of the late nineties, some of its best years came in the first decade of the new millennium, beginning with 2001, when Hero Honda became the world's largest producer of two-wheelers.

The year 2006 was a significant one, for various reasons. On one hand, it marked the golden jubilee of Hero Cycles. Sales of bicycles had crossed the 100 million mark and those of motorcycles, 15 million. On the other, it was the first time that the business papers began to speculate whether Bajaj had a shot at overtaking Hero during a particular quarter's performance, when sales dipped. There was no way my father and Pawan were going to let that happen. We doubled down on our marketing and preserved both our brand equity and market share. All through the 2000s, Hero Honda furiously continued to roll out new models of motorcycles and widen its lead.

* *

My father earned awards and accolades throughout his life, but the most prestigious ones came in a bunch in the 1990s. In 2005, he received the Padma Bhushan. It was testimony to the high esteem in which he was held by the corporate world and one that was publicly articulated by Prime Minister Manmohan Singh. That year, he achieved a long-standing ambition when the first Hero scooter, dubbed the 100 cc Pleasure and consciously aimed at women, hit the roads. (A few years previously, Hero Motors had tied up with Aprilia of Italy to make scooters and co-branded vehicles, including heavy-duty motorcycles, but it hadn't taken off.)

Looking back, Hero's long tenure with Honda was clearly an exception, and not the rule. In 1998–99, Honda's tie-up with the Firodias ended and it launched its own scooter, the Activa, in the following year. Others, like the Nandas of Escorts, the Sundarams of TVS and Bajaj broke up with their foreign partners much earlier. I think it would be safe to say that Hero Honda might have gone a similar way, had it not been for my father's towering personality.

The Hero–Honda partnership was reaffirmed in 2004 and lived on to witness its silver jubilee in 2009. Certainly, it was the most successful of Honda's joint ventures in India but like all good things, it had to come to an end.

A year later, in 2010, Hero and Honda parted ways amicably and the partners would now be competitors. Technically, we could have used the Hero–Honda brand until 2014, but preferred to replace it with Hero as soon as possible. The new avatar, Hero MotoCorp, was unveiled in 2011 with considerable fanfare.

In the first decade of the new millennium, as my father gradually handed over the reins of Hero MotoCorp, Pawan came into his own. As I mentioned earlier, he was meticulous and detail-oriented by nature, and he rarely shied away from taking tough calls. This part of his personality helped him efficiently put together, often brick by brick, the new superstructure that Hero MotoCorp required after the parting with Honda.

He introduced a new culture of performance and accountability. Hero Honda had naturally imbibed the Honda way of doing things for many decades and the Japanese imprint, as well as the best practices that my father and uncles put in place, was quite visible, whether it related to choosing technology, introducing shop floor practices, managing the supply chain, dealing with channel partners and sourcing components.

Pawan kept the essence of this system intact, but also brought in American and European thinking and practices at Hero MotoCorp, which he believed would be essential if Hero MotoCorp had to become a global leader in terms of footprint and culture, and not just volume. To a great extent, Pawan's attempts to create a new global and next-generation avatar of the family flagship enterprise seems to be working; even eight years after the separation, Hero MotoCorp remains the overwhelming leader in India's two-wheeler market despite Honda's increased interest and commitment to its Indian operations.

Meanwhile, Hero Cycles, which had become the world's largest manufacturer of bicycles in 1986, has continued to consolidate that position. From being a one-model company, it began producing a range of specialized bicycles, which offered higher margins. In 2002, we tied up with National Bicycle Industries (part of the Matsushita Group) to manufacture high-end bicycles, for which demand was growing at a much faster pace than that of regular bicycles.

As I mentioned earlier, the growth of Hero Cycles came at a cost to our own bicycle component business. The bicycle business relied on an efficient and low-cost supply chain. Our component-making companies had become so large that their fixed costs went up to the point that competitiveness was undermined.

Now, it was understood that whenever a company buying from or supplying to a family owned enterprise was set up, all parties concerned would have the freedom to make purchases or supply goods wherever it was financially most viable for them to do so. The Hero Group culture precluded taking the kind of shortcuts that smaller enterprises outside were wont to adopt, which meant that entities like Rockman and Highway were no longer competitive by the turn of the millennium.

To add to our problems, in 2003–04 we experienced labour unrest for the first time in our history. The strike at our facilities was part of the general unrest among industrial workers in Punjab. Labour unions had discovered virgin territory among the thousands of small businesses and lakhs of workers in the state. We always had workers' committees at our facilities, where grievances were voiced and addressed, so unionization caught us unawares. My father and the other elders were naturally perturbed, and asked me to play the role of troubleshooter.

Captain Amarinder Singh had taken over as chief minister of Punjab in 2002 and as I knew him from the Doon School, I sought an appointment. My brother Suman who was heading Rockman and Umesh, my cousin who helmed Highway, accompanied me. I explained that continuing the manufacture of cycle parts made no sense. The companies would die and the workers would lose their jobs. It would be far better to reskill the workers and convert the companies to the manufacture of auto components, for which there was a demand. Rockman had already had a motorcycle chains division since 1996.

He asked me to make a presentation to the top rung of the state bureaucracy, which I did. It was the first and, as far as I know, the only case in which two units were given permission to shut down. Rockman Cycles became Rockman Industries and Highway Cycles became Highway Industries.

* *

In 2004–05, my father and I inadvertently made history. I became CII president, which made us the only father and son to have headed that august organization. Another father-son first was the Sir Jehangir Ghandy medal, which my father received in 2000 and I, in 2015. In fact, from 2000 onwards, there would be barely any year when my father was not honoured with at least one award. In 2004, in addition to a couple of lifetime achievement awards, my father – who had never been to college – was given an honorary doctorate from Benares Hindu University (BHU).

By this time, the group had diversified into commodity exports, financial services, IT and IT-enabled services, insurance, renewable energy, real estate and so on. We even had a utility bill collection and retail service, dubbed Easybill. GenNext of the Munjal family was firmly in place and there were no less than twenty-one Munjals in key positions in the group. Our extended family, of course, was much larger. My father would often say with pride that forty of our former employees had become successful entrepreneurs.

9

Continuity in Diversity and Transition

'Chhote Bauji is waiting for you,' I was told as I walked into the office at the Hero Cycles factory in Ludhiana on a wintry evening in 2005. Sure enough, uncle Om Prakash was in his customary chair, looking a shade more sombre than usual. I touched his feet, then sat down and waited for him to broach a subject that I knew he found rather uncomfortable.

Some eight months earlier, I had tentatively broached the idea of restructuring the ownership of the Hero Group with my father and uncles. As gently as possible, I tried to walk them through the challenges of generational transition in family owned global businesses, such as ours. I gave them several examples of the self-interest and egotism that all too often, set brother against brother and father against son.

In the recent past, I pointed out, public feuds between patriarchs and sons and between siblings of hitherto close-knit families had become a staple of news headlines and a cautionary tale for family owned businesses. At a time when acrimony had become the norm in several of India's largest business houses, the Hero Group stood apart. It was distinguished by the harmony between all the Munjal scions, which contributed to the orchestration of the entire group's business activities.

From the very inception of the business, it was understood that each of the elder Munjal siblings equally owned the business; they would not have had it any other way. When my uncle Dayanand passed away, his son, Vijay was automatically accorded the status of a senior member of the group and family. As the group expanded, promoter holdings in the various companies were structured to ensure a balanced equity between the family units; each brother had the same amount of say and commanded the same degree of respect within the various group entities and in the family, even though each business was run independently.

I have delivered lectures on family run businesses in management schools and universities around the world on numerous occasions. My audience would often cite the Hero Group as an example of a 'family that eats together, stays together' or in our case, 'works together'. They would invariably ask how we managed it.

The question is best addressed in cultural and historical terms. The uncommon, indeed unique, congeniality that has been our hallmark is based entirely on the exceptional bond between members of the Munjal family. Forged in times of extreme adversity, during the upheavals of the Partition and post-Partition years, the attachment between the siblings went beyond the usual Punjabi sense of filial bonhomie. In the long and occasionally hazardous journey from the by-lanes of Kamalia and the tiny spare parts shop in Ludhiana, to the multifarious corporate offices established across the world; all through the operose decades of running the Hero Group, they had supported each other in the face of overwhelming odds, never giving up and never losing sight of what was truly important: people, relationships and family.

Our elders instilled in us their values and sprituality, which they had inherited from their elders. In fact, among members of the second generation and their spouses, Anju Bhabhi, Renu Bhabhi and many others have taken the mantle of spirituality and public service from their in-laws, and are actively involved in the *Arya Samaj* and other social activities. Similarly, my wife Mukta and daughter Shefali spend time with charities involving slum children and the homeless of Delhi, and in supporting the arts, crafts and artisans.

If ever there was a difference of opinion, we deferred to our elders; their word was law. So deep was the understanding between them that if one of the brothers took a decision, the others owned it, no questions asked. If one of them spoke, it was as if all of them had spoken.

They epitomized grace and empathy. I can state with absolute confidence that if a disparaging remark was directed at any member of the family, they would mitigate the criticism by citing extenuating circumstances. The person concerned must have had this or that problem, they would rationalize, and in their scheme of things, no one in the entire system should be made to look or feel bad. Of course, this did not stop them from roundly ticking off the erring individual, or commenting and dispensing advice when course-correction was necessary, but it was all effectuated with dignity and good humour, so that no one was humiliated or made to feel small.

Yet where there had been four, there were now more than a score. Three generations of Munjals were actively involved in the business. Surely the best way to keep misunderstandings at bay and the family together was to allow a measure of self-determination, albeit within the parameters of the value system inculcated in all of us by the patriarchs.

As I'd expected, they reacted with consternation to my proposed restructuring. The very concept must have appeared to fly in the face of the 'Family First' principle they had consistently followed in their personal and professional lives. They pointed out that what I was suggesting effectively implied a partition of the Hero Group, assets and all. It went against everything the family had ever stood for and believed in up until that point.

In short, they didn't like it, not one bit. This business had been built to provide for the family and, in their minds, splitting it could well end up undermining their legacy. They said the businesses were doing well by and large, most of the family got along well together, so it didn't make sense to look at restructuring at this juncture. I agreed with them, and explained that in most cases, family restructuring took place due to a fight amongst family members or when the business was doing badly. It was only the sensible and proactive ones who would consider this as a future-proofing when the going was good.

I left it at that as I knew they would mull over it, weigh the pros and cons and discuss it between themselves and, then, with our respective mothers and aunts.

They came back to me in about six weeks, seeking further details on the mechanism of the restructuring and the nature of the potential outcomes. I explained what I had seen, or garnered from around the world – businesses sustained over generations tended to be proactive, rather than reactive when it came to family settlements; invariably, family partitions affected in the midst of conflict led to misunderstandings.

As I had anticipated, I spent the next few months fielding calls from both the patriarchs. They asked me probing questions on various aspects of the business, the performance of individual group entities, the professional reputations of each member of the family and a host of other details as they wanted to take an informed decision. I could see that their primary concern was the potential impact of such a move on intra-family and inter-family dynamics.

My father and uncles were able to wrap their heads around the restructuring proposal fairly quickly. They had never turned away from a difficult decision in the past, so they confronted the truth, no matter how unpalatable it seemed. I remember the incredible resolve and courage that my father showed as he came to terms with the loss of his eldest son. I knew, therefore, he would square up to the reality of a succession plan that involved division of the group assets.

Yet the elders took some convincing. I knew they were not opposed to the idea, otherwise they wouldn't have kept calling me with long lists of questions.

That evening in Ludhiana, I could see that my uncle Om Prakash was finally ready to come on board. He told me that he had discussed the matter with my father and uncle Satyanand, and had come to the conclusion that it was not just inevitable but the best way forward. In fact, he sounded quite determined and enthusiastic, and insisted that we conduct the process efficiently. I then suggested that it would be best for the elders to take the detailed decision of the actual restructuring as the family culture would ensure that their advice was followed without being questioned. For months, thereafter, the elders considered various permutations for the restructuring, and even co-opted two of our advisors.

* *

It gradually became obvious to the elders that the restructuring could not be implemented quickly. A long and arduous process of ideation, conversation, reflection and, perhaps, persuasion and conciliation, lay ahead. After all, there were at least a couple of dozen stakeholders involved and many more who were indirectly invested in the outcome.

The next eight to ten months were a trying period for the elders. For them, it was a traumatic decision to divide up an enterprise that they had set up with a complete sense of togetherness. The elders felt both upset and frustrated with the process, and uncle Om Prakash had a second serious and sombre conversation with me on the same subject. He said that it was turning out to be a much tougher task for the elders to divide something that they had built with their heart and soul. So, he asked me to take responsibility and work with the advisors, one of whom was Pradeep Dinodia, who is now on the board of Hero MotoCorp. 'Since you have a good relationship with the entire family, you should take the responsibility to coordinate this on our behalf,' uncle Om Prakash said.

Over the course of the next one year, we, the second generation, began to hold exploratory discussions with various members of the famly, to try and ascertain each one's aspirations and inclinations. From time to time, I reported back to the family elders, who would sign off on the actual restructuring. All three were still quite active in the business, although uncle Om Prakash was approaching eighty and the other two had crossed that milestone years earlier. We had consciously avoided setting a time frame for the preparatory groundwork, even to myself. I knew my father and uncles would want it done right, not fast. I started slowly, just chipping away at the edges of the idea. There was no question of involving outsiders in the discussions. A few family friends and advisors did get involved, but neither the elders, nor any of us, publicly disclosed what was happening, or why.

In fact, this was one of the first family restructuring exercises that was publicized only after the process was over. Pursuant to the initial discussions, a certain clarity was achieved on actualizing the restructuring, to ensure that it was fair to each individual and productive for all. In effect, the restructuring aimed to create a win-win for both the family and the business.

For the next four years, the nitty-gritty was worked out, a little bit at a time. It took many, many iterations and rounds of confabulation. One reason for this was the desire to be completely compliant with the rules, laws and regulations governing all the businesses and these transactions. Plus, at the slightest hint that matters could take an unpleasant turn, we pulled back. The underlying principle was that no one should feel uncomfortable, or short-changed.

We created a small in-house group, with one member representing each of the four Munjal families, with a professional to support and oversee the process for each family. For example, in our family, Rohit Chanana and others of my team were involved. Limiting the interface to four made it easier and quicker to discuss ideas and arrive at solutions. We were conscious that family solidarity apart, a messy and noisy division would prove detrimental to the business and, just as importantly, the family's interest. If various members of the family were to start pulling in different directions, market confidence in the Hero Group could have been eroded.

The complexity of the proposed restructuring cannot be overstated. In all, there were thirty-two separate operating business entities, and each one of them had distinct compliance requirements. At least seven of them were on a global scale and (as described earlier) most of them were closely interlinked. In the interests of continuity and ensuring the least disruption, we decided that it would be preferable if vendors, employees and dealers continued to deal with the person who was already in place as the CEO. The logic: it would cause the least disruption and ensure the ongoing success of the business. In effect, the consensus was that the ownership of a business should be transferred to the person or the family member who was already operationally involved and considered the face of that particular enterprise, as far as practical and possible.

Once the patriarchs were on board, they thought further ahead than we did. They decided that if any branch of the family so desired, they could choose to simultaneously effect a succession for the next generation as well. Uncle Satyanand's family decided in favour, as did that of uncle Dayanand.

Even as we were putting our restructuring plan in place, during the years 2005–10, several notable business houses were going through angst-ridden internecine battles and in some cases, bucketloads of dirty linen were washed in public. We were confounded and not a little shocked at this undignified display of acrimony; it made us even more determined to keep our revamp of ownership as harmonious and private as possible.

* *

In our case, there were no external or internal triggers forcing the family into a division of assets. It was a proactive and prudent step, to pre-empt the possibility of conflicts in the future. The thirty-odd business family break-ups in the 1980s and even thereafter, had mostly been bitter. Global research studies, including those by management consultants and research firms, show that 94 per cent of family businesses rarely survive beyond the third generation. In many cases they tend to implode as a result of infighting. Only 6 per cent remain intact or make a smooth transition by finding ways to thrive thereafter. One of the key features of this small group of firms has been the ability to distinguish between ownership and management. We were obviously determined to be part of that 6 per cent.

Succession planning was not in vogue, even in the 1990s. This may have been a cultural hangover from the early twentieth century, when joint families were the main source of capital for Indian companies. What made our succession planning even more challenging was the complicated business structure we had been compelled to build, thanks to the restrictive policy environment that prevailed, especially in the 1970s.

After the managing agency system was abolished in 1970 and the MRTP Act introduced in 1969, companies with assets of ₹100 crore or more came under severe scrutiny. They needed the government's approval for any major expansion of production capacity, diversification of existing activities, establishment of interconnected companies, or for amalgamations, mergers or takeovers, in whole or part. The ostensible aim of the Act was to ensure that wealth was not concentrated in the hands of the few.

Yet in the process, it created an incredibly difficult business environment not just for us, but for entrepreneurs and industrial groups across India. Till the end of March 1990, 1,854 undertakings had been registered under the MRTP Act. Of these, 1,787 undertakings belonged to large industrial houses and the remaining sixty-seven were dominant undertakings.

The cap on MRTP firms implied that large firms were rigidly shackled, while small-sized firms were relatively free of government regulation. Thus, promoters could expand only by setting up multiple small companies controlled through cross-holdings in order to remain compliant with the regulations. So it was with the Hero Group.

My father and uncles would often recall the tribulations they faced during the MRTP era, in terms of knocking at the doors of government authorities to seek approval for every major company decision. This absurd paradigm continued right up to the Industrial Policy of 1991, which scrapped the assets limit for MRTP companies.

* *

My father and uncles were determined that while the aspirations of different members of the family should be accommodated as far as possible in the restructuring, it should also be fair to stakeholders outside the family as well. Along with regulatory compliance, they wanted to protect individual and institutional shareholders and ensure the businesses did not suffer. From their perspective, the business was an organic and sensitive entity, subject to mood swings and fluctuating health, mirroring human physiology.

After the draft proposal had been discussed by the family elders and members of the second generation, a number of top legal and technical minds were requested to vet the procedure and documentation. Following their approval, Satish Bansal, the family's statutory auditor and tax advisor, was asked to create the final filings. Fifty year old Satish was a third-generation chartered accountant, carrying forward the legacy of his grandfather, B.D. Bansal, and founder of the eminent chartered accountancy firm, B.D. Bansal & Company. The venerable gentleman, who set up his CA firm in 1949, had handled the Munjal accounts from Hero's inception, and then passed the baton on to his son, R.K. Bansal, who handed it to his son, Satish, who now works with his son, Sumit.

We had briefly considered handing over the assignment to two leading chartered accountancy firms in Mumbai. My father had even spoken with them, but realized that they didn't quite understand where we were coming from. The kind of resources they insisted would be required for the exercise appeared excessive. They made it seem far more complicated than it was; nor could they understand a family where some members were willing to sacrifice self-interest to keep the peace. At one point, my father told me, 'Please be fair and equitable ... and if anyone is not happy, then you give them something out of my share.' I assured him that while I appreciated the sentiment, there was no reason why such a situation should arise.

The elders were finally on board and one day in 2009, they called Satish to a meeting in Delhi. Some of us, members of the second generation, were present. The elders told Satish two things: first, that the brothers were on the same page, as were their children; second, that they wanted the succession issue settled within their lifetimes, so that each member of the family could live up to his or her potential. I suspect that Satish was a little bowled over by the enormity of the task, but agreed at once that it was an excellent idea.

Satish got down to work and in him we were assured of a thorough professional with a personal touch. His first step was to benchmark, or evaluate, the assets of the entire group. Over the next few months, with inputs from us, he drew up a mammoth family settlement agreement running into many, many chapters. To cut a very long story short, we managed to partition a multi-billion dollar group in an entirely cashless settlement, without an apparent glitch being visible to the outside world. It was unique, in that such a large exercise, both in terms of monetary value and the number of people involved, had been by and large kept out of the public eye.

This was pretty much in line with our philosophy and media policy. Regardless of whether the media wrote something positive or negative about us, we held our peace and maintained an amicable relationship with them. So we never gave statements or news bytes about what we wanted to do, or were going to do. We would normally send out press statements only after the event was over. Most of us continue to follow this policy till today.

We did make the separation public post facto, but only because we had to, as five of our companies were listed. In fact that was the first the world at large heard about the restructuring of the group. It quickly became the talk of corporate India, for the sheer finesse with which it was accomplished. I received calls from several business schools and consultancies to deliver talks on the succession exercise, but refused most of them. I did, however, speak to a few select family friends who needed advice.

* *

My father was at the helm of Hero Honda Motors and so, it was decided that the stake held by the Munjals should go to him and his family (Suman, Pawan, I, and my late brother's family). As we were also handling Rockman, Hero Corporate Service, Hero ITES, Hero Mindmine, Hero Soft and Easybill, we received control of these companies as well.

Uncle Om Prakash and family received ownership of Hero Cycles, whereas uncle Satyanand's family took over Majestic Auto, Highway, Munjal Auto and Munjal Showa. My cousin Vijay already held charge of Hero Exports, while his brother Ashok was looking after Sunbeam, and these entities were formally transferred to them. The remaining entities were also transferred in the same manner.

Family members who held shares in group companies, transferred their stakes to the respective business heads. The exercise, which started with unlisted firms, culminated with shares of the five listed firms – Hero Honda, Munjal Showa, Majestic Auto, Munjal Auto and Shivam Autotech – being transferred through a series of stock market transactions.

The employees, suppliers and clients of each of the group companies faced no changes. For example, Rockman Industries continued to be a key Hero MotoCorp vendor supplying chains and wheels, as were Munjal Showa, Munjal Auto, Shivam Autotech and Sunbeam Auto, control of which had passed to the Dayanand and Satyanand Munjal family units.

All those involved agreed that but for the principles and values instilled by the patriarchs, that over time had permeated the entire group, the division could not have gone through, at least not in the smooth manner that it did. Even though some of the members may not have been completely happy, there was little heartburn or rebellion over perceived injustice in the distribution of assets.

Another conundrum was the family trusts, which ran various educational institutions and social service initiatives. Obviously, all the organizations under the umbrella of the trusts were non-profits. Someone had to supervise their functioning, because our name and credibility were at stake. Satish asked whether we wanted to run them independently, or as a family. A united community service platform, he pointed out, could bolster our image and further assure the markets that all was well; the Hero entities would stand together, apportionment of ownership regardless.

To mark the conclusion of the restructuring process, the elders mooted a get-together of the entire family, which, as on many family occasions, was hosted by uncle Om Prakash. It was to celebrate the fact that we had passed a difficult milestone with dignity and grace. The patriarchs addressed the gathering. Essentially, they said it was 'a continuation of the family in a different form'. It had been done, they added, to ensure that individuals had 'more freedom of choice while continuing to remain an integral part of the larger family'.

As far as the optics were concerned, the group remained largely unchanged. In fact, some of us continue to serve on or even chair, boards of companies owned by our cousins, brothers or nephews, in which we now have no ownership. I am on the boards of Rockman Industries which is under Suman, and Shivam Autotech, which is run by Yogesh's son Neeraj. Similarly, Suman sits on the board of Hero Corporate Service and Hero Steels, which I manage; Yogesh sits on the board of Hero Cycles, and so on.

It was an emotional moment for all of us and particularly for my father and his siblings. The manner in which the partition had been effected, over five years, had put their apprehensions at rest. They could let go the reins in the comforting knowledge that their legacy would survive, at least for the foreseeable future. The way my father saw it, they had built a firm foundation for the family. Now, it was time to allow subsequent generations to venture out of their comfort zones, exercise their creativity and grow.

That was precisely what my father had done all through his life. His was the DNA of an explorer and a pioneer; he had opened up new avenues of business and institution building by taking big gambles and tackling obstacles with high courage. He had always done what he believed was correct and in the best interests of his family, and left the rest to a higher power.

In the years to come, he would be proved right, as the Munjals diversified into new areas, experimented, expanded, flourished and secured their place in the annals of corporate history.

To a large extent, the philosophy of our forebearers is reflected in our businesses even today. We have endeavoured to protect the core of their value system, that people are the key to our business, not just products and parts.The third generation of our dealers and suppliers still work with us, as do the fourth generation of our auditors! Some of the entities look and feel like the earlier days, others feel a little different, but broadly, most still follow the principles laid down by the Brothers Munjal.

10

Spiritual Roots and Societal Impact

For as long as I can remember, the *havan* has been part of the daily morning ritual in most of the Munjal homes. This is how the days always began when we were home in our younger days: with the warmth of a fire, the fragrance of burning *ghee* (clarified butter) and *samigri*[11] and the rejuvenating effects of the early morning sun; the white trails of smoke curling upwards in puffs, the family sitting cross-legged around the *havan kund* and the room reverberating with mantras and spiritual wisdom.

---

[11] A sacred offering in *havan* (a holy fire) after chanting the mantra each time along with *ghee* and other items.

The ceremony was both a celebration and an offering of gratitude to the Almighty in the classic traditions of the *Arya Samaj*. Most of our homes have a *yagyashala*[12] and when mantras are recited, healing vibrations are said to emanate from the earth, dispelling diseases and negative energies. It is a rite we have followed religiously, from the time we all lived in a single lane in Ludhiana. But the practice did not begin there. It started much earlier, when our elders were still young boys in Kamalia and the idea of Partition had not been conceived.

Social commitment is integral to the tenets of the *Arya Samaj*, but the urge to serve may have been a legacy of our grandmother, Thakuri Devi, a god-fearing woman with strong inclinations towards *samajseva* (social service).

My grandfather, who was on crutches because of debilitating arthritis, firmly believed that his children must be useful members of society. The result was a strong value system whereby success was to be gained in service of others rather than at the expense of others.

What started as an article of faith later translated into action, especially when the Munjal brothers were in a position to make substantial contributions to society. Doubtless, their inclination towards philanthropy stemmed from a deeply spiritual upbringing. It influenced their business decisions and propelled them to adopt and actualize the concept of CSR decades before the term became part of business jargon.

While all the brothers were devout followers of the *Arya Samaj*, it was uncle Satyanand – thanks to his early training at the *gurukul* in Kamalia – who ensured that its tenets and principles were embedded and reflected in the functioning of the business. But to understand what spurred the brothers to serve society, it might be useful to first comprehend the *Arya Samaj* movement and its genesis.

* *

---

12 An enclosure within which a *yagya* is performed.

In April 1875, a *sanyasi* (ascetic) from Tankara in Gujarat, Maharishi Dayanand Saraswati, founded a reform movement to modernize orthodox Hinduism and called it the *Arya Samaj*. It was established as a societal and philosophical movement, rather than a religion. Its aim was to re-establish the primacy of the Vedas, reject idol worship, animal sacrifice, untouchability, child marriage, bias against women, sati, pilgrimages, temple offerings, and a caste system that was based on birth rather than merit. In short, it sought to abolish every form of the deep-rooted malaise that had crept into the religion over centuries. The *Arya Samaj* also introduced the concept of monotheism, promoted inter-caste marriages and tried to improve the lot of widows.

Within this period (1869–1873), Swami Dayanand had already established *gurukuls* (Vedic schools) which stressed Vedic values and culture, *satya* (truth) and the *sanatan dharma* (eternal order). The gurukuls sought to educate boys and girls, and were set up as an improvement over the British education system. A strong subterranean strain of nationalism also pulsated within the Samaj.

In Punjab, the movement took root in 1877, when it was first established in Lahore. From here, it spread quickly and turned into a mass movement in northern and western India. One reason for its swift growth in Punjab was the pressure that Hindu identity faced from other religious groups like the Singh Sabha (a forerunner of the Akali Dal), Muslim clerics and Christian missionaries.

Early on, leaders like Pandit Lekh Ram and Swami Shraddhanand picked up Swami Dayanand's mantle in Punjab and began to wield a great deal of influence over the North Indian Hindu communities. Pandit Lekh Ram commanded a large following in northern Punjab, especially among urban Hindus. The elder Munjals were among those who came under his influence. Swami Shraddhanand held sway in lower Punjab and western Uttar Pradesh.

Inevitably, tensions between the various competing religious groups ran high. Pandit Lekh Ram, in particular, had regular run-ins with the Ahmadiyya community. The friction eventually culminated in the assassination of both leaders – Pandit Lekh Ram in 1897 and Swami Shraddhanand in 1926.

The latter's death devastated his disciples. Uncle Satyanand, who was born in May 1917 and was nine years old at the time, recalled: 'There was a pall of gloom in the Munjal household and no food was served that day. It was as if a close member of the family had died. We were not the only ones who did not eat that day.'

The *Arya Samaj* would always hold a prominent place in uncle Satyanand's life. His devotion was so great that the Samaj feted him for his 'sincerity and commitment' when he was just seventeen and was living in Quetta. The award remained one of his most prized possessions; he would occasionally fish it out and show it to the youngsters in the family.

The only time my uncle lost touch with the movement was during the unrest preceding the Partition. Yet once he reached Delhi and life returned to an even keel, he renewed his connections within the Samaj.

Later, when he moved to Ludhiana and joined the business, new avenues opened up and uncle Satyanand now had the resources to make a difference and the backing to plunge into the Samaj's social work. My father and uncle Om Prakash, more focused on the business end of things, nevertheless gave him all the support he needed for his spiritual forays. My father and uncle Om Prakash supported him completely and took care of all the financial requirements, no questions asked.

'Mahatma Munjal', as my uncle Satyanand was known, was a man of strong spiritual leanings, and did research on the Vedas every day. He remained an active member of the Samaj all his life and became a leading figure in the Dayanand Anglo-Vedic (DAV) Public School movement and helped establish a network of educational institutions for the Samaj and also became a member of the *Arya Samaj* Sarvdeshic Sabha and the Tankara Trust.

His most notable philanthropic contributions were the primary and higher education projects that he set up across north India in my grandfather's name. Today, there are seven Bahadur Chand Munjal

(BCM) Arya schools in Ludhiana and a BCM College of Education which provides teacher's training. The latter was set up in 1998 and became the first institute of higher education in Punjab to run on a self-financing model, reflecting the Munjal philosophy of setting up institutions that are not for profit, yet financially viable and sustainable.

Although uncle Satyanand took care of most of the day-to-day work at these schools, my father and uncle Om Prakash were also closely involved in the projects. The initiative in Punjab was later extended and carried forward throughout the NCR, by the Raman Kant Munjal Foundation. Subsequently, schools were set up in Haridwar through the BML Munjal Foundation.

In addition to setting up the family schools, uncle Satyanand also set up more than twenty *Arya Samaj* establishments in Ludhiana and many more within Punjab and Uttarakhand (a state in North India), assisted by a team of dedicated volunteers. Many of the new *Arya Samaj* institutions are located in the remote, hilly areas of the Garhwal region in Uttarakhand, with poor connectivity and worse infrastructure. Asked how he managed it, he remarked, 'People have a way of becoming what you encourage them to be.'

Despite his spiritual bent of mind, my uncle's outlook towards society was anything but rigid. He believed that 'rigidity chases people away'. My cousin Yogesh once described how deftly his father had handled the rather starchy Swami Vigyananand, one of the spiritual preceptors who frequented their home. My uncle had invited him to survey the English medium co-ed school he had set up. Swamiji did not approve either the fact that the school was open to both genders, or that the medium of instruction was English. Uncle Satyanand dexterously won him over by saying: 'If we hadn't started the school, these children would have gone to a missionary school.' Swamiji thereafter held his peace.

There is no doubt that uncle Satyanand was the moral compass of the family. His mechanical expertise was invaluable, but it was his deeply ingrained sense of social service, often driving him to herculean efforts, which made him special.

After the devastating Chamoli (in the state of Uttarakhand) earthquake in 1999, he led the relief operations in the Himalayan town, with a small band of *Arya Samaj* volunteers. They travelled to the most remote and worst-affected areas, suffering considerable physical hardship, living just as the common people did. He slept on the ground, ate what was available and displayed none of the airs that might have been expected of the chairman of a large industrial house. This practice of volunteering, especially in times of calamity, went on to become an established norm in the group in later years. During the earthquakes in Bhuj, Latur and Uttarkashi, teams from the group, and associated hospitals travelled to the ravaged areas with materials and other support.

Most of our elders are no longer with us today, but this tradition of social service during times of crisis continues to this day. During the devastating Covid19 crisis of 2020, the different arms of the family business went beyond the call of duty in keeping with the family tradition. BML Munjal University offered its 2000-bed hostel as an isolation and treatment ward; family owned ancillary firms distributed meals, dry rations and hygiene kits to people across villages located near project sites while the group's finance arm offered subsidized loan packages to select Covid-impacted businesses. Flagship firm Hero MotoCorp distributed protection wear and ventilators to hospitals and health departments and deployed some of its motorcycles for use as mobile ambulances in rural areas.

Back to my uncles. Uncle Satyanand was regarded as a personage, and a sage, in Ludhiana. People sought his advice, both professional and personal. He would discuss the teachings of the *Arya Samaj* and the importance of detachment from the material world and offered his services wherever they were needed.

Schools were set up where they were needed the most. The BCM School for workers in Ludhiana was inspired by a Hero employee, who complained that his child could not attend the existing school in Shastri Nagar because it was too far away. Uncle Satyanand immediately drew up plans for a school in the workers' colony which turned out to be an excellent institution. One of the alumni, the daughter of a security guard, was a topper in the Punjab board exams in 1987. To her immense joy, the actor and Member of Parliament, Sunil Dutt, took time out just to meet her during his *padyatra* (a long march for a non-violent purpose) from Mumbai to Amritsar in 1987 to restore peace to terrorism-torn Punjab.

As an incentive to the workers and their children, Hero offers subsidized education to toppers, a practice that has been in place for a number of years. In 2019, in this school, the first, third and fifth positions in the Board examinations were bagged by children of immigrants from Uttar Pradesh and Bihar who might not even have had access to an education otherwise.

* *

Uncle Satyanand's magnanimity helped him fulfill a long-standing wish, of acquiring for the *Arya Samaj* the house in Tankara (Gujarat) where Maharishi Dayanandji was born. The Samaj had managed to acquire land in the town, but had failed to persuade the owner to part with the house. He cited a sentimental attachment to the property and no amount of pleading could move him.

A high-powered delegation of *Arya Samaj*, of which my uncle and a Member of Parliament were a part, met the then prime minister, Indira Gandhi, requesting her intervention. She courteously heard them out, but gently turned them down. The Munjal family approached the owner directly, asking him to name his price, but he was adamant.

Finally, the Samaj gave up and instead, established a memorial to Swami Dayanand on their land in Tankara and uncle Satyanand eventually became chairman of the Tankara Trust. The state government realized the town's potential as a destination for pilgrimage and began promoting it vigorously as a tourist spot.

As fate would have it, uncle Satyanand's grandson went to Nagpur to pursue a degree in engineering fell in love with a Gujarati college-mate and declared his intention of marrying her. For a conservative Punjabi family, this came as a great shock. Uncle Satyanand brushed aside their parochial sentiments and cajoled the family to be more forward-looking. Being the eldest, he prevailed and the marriage was solemnized.

Serendipitously, it turned out that the bride's maternal grandfather was the proprietor of the very same house that the *Arya Samaj* had tried to acquire: the birthplace of Swami Dayanand. After the marriage, she realized just how important the house was to the Munjals. She spoke to her mother, who in turn, took up the matter with her father.

A few days later, the bride's grandfather arrived at the Munjal home. He brought with him a basket of fruits – and the title to Swamiji's birthplace. He refused to accept monetary compensation. The house and the surrounding land were then transferred to the Tankara Trust. Today, havans are performed in the room where Swami Dayanand was born. My niece's grandfather also handed over the utensils and boxes that had once belonged to Swamiji's family. They are now on display to the public.

Another major contribution that the Munjals made to the Samaj was the establishment of a *gurukul* for girls in Ludhiana. It was by no means simple since special efforts had to be made to ensure the safety of the girls in the hostel, and parents had to be convinced that their daughters would be well looked after. Teachers had to be selected carefully and the curriculum broadened to ensure that girls emerging from the *kanya* (girl) *gurukul* were employable. It was decided that they would graduate high school with a certificate from a recognized board and simultaneously receive training in computers. It was my uncle's pet project; he would stop over on his way to the factory and spend some time there, a practice he continued as long as he lived.

Uncle Satyanand set up several *Arya Samaj* branches called *shakhas* and revived those that had shut down. Once, while opening a *shakha*, he told us how Pandit Lekh Ram had left his ailing son in Peshawar to rush to Payal village near Ludhiana, where a mass conversion to Islam was scheduled. He had boarded the Frontier Mail, which didn't stop at Payal, so he pulled the chain and jumped out, injuring himself in the process. He managed to stop the conversions, but returned to find that he had lost his son.

My uncle led a simple, disciplined life. He knew the Vedas by heart and if he wasn't at the factory or visiting one of his schools (he would rise very early, so as to visit at least one school each day and still reach the factory before everyone else!), he would be in his room studying, reading and researching. Sundays were devoted exclusively to the Samaj. He would spend his evenings explaining Vedic mantras to his followers, taking the trouble to teach them the correct Sanskrit pronunciation.

The younger generation of the family will always remember him for his unconditional love, tolerance and resilience; when his daughter passed away after losing her battle against cancer, he was the one who comforted everybody else.

In 2005, uncle Satyanand toyed with the idea of opting for *vanprastha* (giving up worldly life, and living the life of a hermit, away from home and secluded from family and society), but finally decided that he 'could not leave home'. Swami Satyapati, who was staying with him in Baroda, told him that *vanprastha* was a metaphorical concept. He could observe the principle of detachment, regardless of where he chose to live.

My uncle then took *diksha* (initiation) for *vanprastha*, but continued to work and stay at home. In all the ways that mattered, he became an ascetic. He would return all the gifts offered to him and subsist on one roti and sabzi, no matter how hard we tried to persuade him otherwise.

* *

My father was an active member of Rotary International, the international body that works towards creating welfare and goodwill in society. He had joined the movement in the 1960s and became an active Rotarian at the international as well as local levels. In 1973, he stood as a candidate for governor of the Rotary district encompassing

Punjab, Haryana, Himachal Pradesh, Jammu and Kashmir, Delhi and a substantial part of Uttar Pradesh. The governor's post went to someone else, but it didn't diminish his involvement. He believed in the philosophy of the Bhagavad Gita, one of the holy texts of Hinduism: work and don't worry about rewards.

Four years later, he became the district governor. Despite the fact that Hero's new projects were taking off at the time, he devoted considerable time and energy to the Rotary Club, getting involved in district, zonal and national activities.

Rajendra Saboo, my father's predecessor as district governor, who was also one of his closest friends in Rotary, writes admiringly about my father's role in the Rotary movement: 'His humility and belief in social service became his trademark in human interactions. How can I forget his readiness to donate blood at the blood donation camp I had organized at the Chandigarh Conference? Whenever a project needed monetary support, he'd do his utmost for its success.'

My father was equally passionate about healthcare. After playing an active role in managing the Dayanand Medical College and Hospital at Ludhiana for a number of years, he became its president (a mantle which later passed to me).

The Dayanand Medical College and Hospital was a small medical college and hospital run by the *Arya Samaj*, which ran into trouble with the state government because of pending dues. My father, along with leading citizens of Ludhiana, such as Mr Dhanda and Mr Dheer, and a few others, stepped in and managed to collect enough money to put the institution back on its feet. Admittedly, my father had to top up the funds from his own pocket and he did so cheerfully. The DMCH is now one of the leading medical colleges and hospitals of north India, providing quality care to common citizens. It is known for its support to poor patients who can't afford even moderate levels of pricing.

In 2001, DMCH decided to expand its activities, and the Hero Group offered to help with the funding. A state-of-the-art heart institute was set up to provide world class yet affordable cardiac care.

Until then, one had to rush to Delhi in case of a cardiac emergency. From 140 beds, the Hero DMC Heart Institute has grown into a nearly 200 bed hospital and is considered one of the best cardiac care centres in north India.

In fact, my father's attention to healthcare wasn't restricted to urban centres. He instinctively understood how difficult it was for denizens of villages to travel to urban centres for medical care, so he mooted the idea of a mobile medical service. Subsequently, a Hero van, carrying doctors and medical equipment would treat patients in remote areas of Haryana.

After playing an active role in managing the DMCH at Ludhiana for a number of years, he became its president, a post he held for thirty-two years (the mantle passed to me in 2004).

* *

The family's social footprint expanded considerably after the Raman Kant Munjal Foundation was set up in 1991. For close to three decades, the Foundation has been working with economically challenged communities in Haryana. From organizing mass marriages for poor and differently abled girls, to supporting education and promoting vocational training and skill development, the Foundation's social interventions touch almost every aspect of the beneficiaries' lives. This Foundation is looked after by Renu Munjal, the wife of my late brother.

Today, the Foundation's Asha (Hope) centres cater to the remedial educational needs of children studying in understaffed and inadequate government schools in villages. In addition to strengthening the educational base of village children, these centres also organize extracurricular activities which include sports, music, art, good habits, health and hygiene – all aimed at shaping the overall personality of students from villages.

Teachers at these centres are appointed from within the village and trained by a proficient foundation volunteer. The students are assessed twice in a session, through written and oral examinations and a record of their progress is maintained. The Foundation also provides scholarships to Asha-trained girls from underprivileged backgrounds, which enable them to study at the Raman Vidya Mandir in Dharuhera. Affiliated to the Central Board of Secondary Education (CBSE), it is an English medium school that began with two rooms and a 100 children, and has since grown into one of the largest schools in the region.

The forty Asha centres scattered across thirty-four villages in Dharuhera, site of the first Hero Honda factory, function on the principles of sustainability, inclusiveness and progressive growth. From 1993 onwards, they have run vocational and skill enhancement programmes in the villages around Dharuhera, Manesar, Pataudi, Rewari and Bhiwadi. The Hamari Asha programmes aim to foster economic independence among women who are taught how to make various products like jute bags, candles, *diyas* (earthen oil lamps), bags and other handicrafts that are marketed through the Hero ecosystem.

The Foundation has also devised diploma courses in sewing and cutting, that enable women to either run their own boutiques or to find employment in garment-manufacturing units. Those who are unable to reach the main centre because of transportation constraints can attend a satellite centre, typically located within walking distance of a village cluster. Several thousand women have already been trained and are either self-employed or have found jobs in garment manufacturing units in the Gurgaon–Dharuhera–Manesar belt.

A number of social interventions that the family undertook were and continue to be carried out through village-level NGOs or by involving local communities to manage the operational aspects, while remaining actively involved only at the strategic level. In some projects, the family has remained active at both levels.

Hero's engagement in the social sector was primarily driven by the patriarchs' connect with people. If they had the wherewithal to improve the lives of people, be it access to education, potable water, healthcare or job opportunities, they felt it was their responsibility to do so. The Munjal family also became involved in greening projects across multiple levels from the early days, as part of a deep commitment to the environment. As an unintended but welcome consequence, our family won an enormous amount of goodwill amongst the communities in the vicinity of our workplaces through these initiatives.

In many parts of the Hero Group, both the businesses and family members are involved in multiple social initiatives covering a wide range of subjects. Today, the next two generations of Munjals are trying to uphold the legacy of social service and putting their own stamp on social outreach programmes. Rockman Industries has set up Mission Parivartan, an integrated rural development project that includes rural infrastructure development, education and skill development. Hero Corporate Service is actively involved in hunger alleviation and shelter creation programmes in Delhi. Over the years, many of the previously established programmes have been scaled up and replicated elsewhere. For instance, several more Bahadur Chand Munjal schools have been set up, notably in Haryana and Uttarakhand.

Hero MotoCorp has set up road-safety riding schools across India as part of its mission to minimize road accidents in India, which rank among the highest in the world. The company has also partnered with police departments across India and provided them with scooters for their women police officers, thereby enabling them to discharge their duties more efficiently. It has also initiated *Hamari Pari*, an initiative targeted towards girls aged 6+ from underprivileged sections.

In most of the social projects that we undertake, our organizations partner with local NGOs or members of the community. However, we do not absolve ourselves of responsibility and ensure that at least one family member actively oversees the projects.

For example, in the 1990s and 2000s, I enjoyed anchoring our family's involvement in the greening of Ludhiana, in partnership with the local civic agencies. Our objective has been to make the bustling, overcrowded and polluted city more habitable and sustainable through better management of traffic, maintenance of public spaces like parks and efficient waste management, and also to ensure that these practices became an integral part of the city's master plan.

My social and cultural consciousness first found expression in the Ludhiana Sanskritik Samagam – a non-profit organization we set up in the city in 1999 to sensitize the citizens of a business and commerce-driven city to the joys of art and culture.

At a more personal level, my wife, my daughter and I brought our long-cherished dream to fruition in 2015, when we set up the Serendipity Arts Foundation (SAF) to bring back patronage to the arts and also to preserve, foster and develop the creativity, skills and artisanal legacy of artists and communities in South Asia and make them accessible to the public.

The SAF holds an annual Serendipity Arts Festival at Panaji in Goa and, at the time of writing, four editions had been held. The 2019 edition of the festival brought a footfall of over 450,000 visitors. Set in multiple venues along the Mandovi river, this eight-day festival in December showcases music, dance, theatre, visual arts, crafts, photography and culinary arts in an interdisciplinary format. It brings together iconic curators, diverse practitioners from various sections of society and creates new modes of employment.

I have chosen not to connect our foundation with the family name, as this is not essential; connecting it to the family's values and principles of creating livelihoods and skill development is far more important.

Responsible businesses are those that give purpose as much weight as the pursuit of profit. I would like to believe that our desire to create social impact alongside profitable businesses is based on the beliefs, values and best practices set by our elders. The idea of using profit-seeking investments to bring about social and environmental good is slowly catching the imagination of the corporate world, but in our case, this approach started many decades ago.

11

The Making of Brand Hero

The 'hero' archetype is common to most cultures and exemplifies dependability, strength and selflessness. Psychologists have said that all of us have an inner hero, which we channel from time to time and, thus, the 'hero' figure resonates with us across all geographies and demographics.

It follows that building the Hero brand should therefore have been a breeze, more so because every product that rolled out of the Munjal factories emphasized soundness and reliability. This wasn't of course, the case. A brick-by-brick effort and enormous toil over the decades created the brand equity Hero enjoys today. It figures in every list of the most trusted and valued Indian brands and the logo in all its various avatars is recognizable in some fifty countries across the globe.

Yet emotional associations with Brand Hero extend beyond the narrow attributes of the company, its logo, its products or its leadership position. In the first decade of the new millennium, independent studies carried out by the Boston Consulting Group (BCG) on customer and other stakeholder perceptions revealed that Hero as an organization enjoyed strong public support and was seen as one that possessed a modern global mindset. At the same time, it was perceived as a quintessentially Indian company with commensurate values and traits. In the minds of those surveyed, Hero stood for qualities such as 'Respect for the family'; 'The Spirit of India' and 'Spirituality'. It was also perceived as an organization that sought to ensure happiness for all stakeholders.

These perceptions about Brand Hero didn't evolve overnight, nor were they conjured through smart marketing. They evolved organically, from the closely held beliefs nurtured by my father and uncles and the examples they set at work and at home and in their personal interactions. Effectively, over time, these values and practices became the attributes of the brand itself, and in this chapter, I have tried – with the aid of people who were actively involved in the company at the time – to capture some of the human and emotional experiences that sculpted and honed Brand Hero.

By the early 1980s, the Munjal brothers, through their learnings and experiences, understood the truth behind the old marketing epigram, 'the manufacturer makes a product, the consumer buys a brand'. The Hero bicycle was a workhorse, with a reputation for consistency of quality, low maintenance and durability among consumers and dealers alike. In subsequent years, through the Hero Honda motorcycle, the company had divined the kind of commuter vehicle India needed – and found a way to manufacture the best possible product at the least possible price. It was increasingly felt that a strong brand would be a value addition, in terms of commanding customer loyalty and protection against competition.

Hero's foray into advertising had begun on a quiet note with National Publicity, a Delhi-based firm owned by a distant family connection. The proprietor introduced uncle Om Prakash to a freelance film-maker by the name of Harish Oberoi and these two highly creative people clicked.

Harish wrote a jingle for him and shot an ad film around it. The clip ran in cinema halls, then the most popular mode of audio-visual advertising (VCRs were few and far between and cinema was the most widespread form of entertainment). The Hero Cycles promotional film, *Chale Hawa ki Chaal* (Rides like the wind) trilled melodiously before every film and was an instant hit. The power of advertising had transformed the Hero bicycle into a veritable Pegasus, giving people 'wings to fly'.

Having realized the power of advertising as a tool for market outreach, the Munjal brothers now decided on an image-makeover that could turn Hero into a household name and began hunting for the sharpest minds in the ad world. Uncle Om Prakash asked around and was told of an advertising virtuoso by the name of Nikhil Nehru, who haunted the by-lanes of Jhandewalan near central Delhi.

A call was placed to Nehru, then the head of Hindustan Thompson Associates (HTA) in Delhi. The agency had earlier handled the Atlas Speedomatic account, with indifferent results. The ad industry had not yet addressed its creative skills to bicycles and two-wheelers. HTA dispatched two young men, Colvyn Harris and Sunil Gupta (who eventually went on to head HTA in India), to meet with Om Prakash Munjal. They had already been vetted by K.V. Suri, who was my father's right-hand man in Delhi.

Gupta has described his encounter with the Brothers Munjal in a book, *Living on the Edge*. He writes: 'As events of great significance are wont to do, Hero entered my life very quietly, almost nondescriptly. As likely protagonists in a love affair (for it can be called nothing short of that for me), we were as suited to each other as *dal makhni* with noodles, but I have no qualms in saying here and now that as clients go, very few gave me as much professional satisfaction and personal affection as they.'

Gupta met O.P. Munjal at the Hero office at Kundan Mansions near Delite Cinema on Asaf Ali Road and was given to understand that the company wanted to outstrip its competition (notably Atlas Cycles). To begin with, my uncle was a little fazed by HTA's heavy charges but decided to take a chance on them.

Culturally, the Hero and HTA teams seemed to be like chalk and cheese.

The HTA team struggled with Hindi and were taken aback by the absence of a marketing department at Hero Cycles. The warm and congenial atmosphere of the Hero office, the deference with which employees and younger members of the family addressed the patriarchs and the paternal affection with which they responded, must have been a bit of a culture shock. They were particularly impressed by the sensitivity of the staunchly vegetarian Munjals in laying out a non-vegetarian spread for their guests!

Gupta gives an evocative description of his first encounter with my father, the 'paterfamilias': 'He was infinitely more serious and almost stern in his manner. O.P. kept referring to him as Bade Bhai Saab or Bade Bhrata Ji.'

Their very first campaign, for Hero Majestic, was a flop. Neither uncle Om Prakash nor my cousins liked it. The ad was not a success, but they decided to give the HTA youngsters another shot. Fortuitously in 1986, a key trade newspaper of the bicycle industry published out of Tokyo, *Japan Cycle*, declared Hero as the largest producer of bicycles in the world. Soon after, the Guinness Book of World Records reported that Hero had set a world record in manufacturing cycles (a spot it has never since relinquished). So, HTA developed a logo incorporating Hero's pole position as a mnemonic: the 'Hero No. 1' logo, which would henceforth appear on all Hero Cycles communications.

My uncle was thrilled with the design and lauded the HTA team: '*Yeh hui na baat. Ab mujhe pata chala ki aap badi agency hain.*' (You've nailed it! Now I can see you are a big agency.) Mike Khanna, CEO of HTA and one of the doyens of the advertising industry, had heard so much about Om Prakash Munjal and his penchant for breaking into urdu *sher o shayari*, that he sought a meeting. Like the Munjals, his family had been displaced by the Partition and this struck an immediate chord.

From then on, Hero and HTA developed a synergy. The youngsters from HTA forged a bond with Ashok Bawa, my uncle's personal assistant and with Mr Rai, who Gupta describes as, 'the genial head of production'. For the final sign-off on the campaigns, of course, my uncle involved four or five people, including my father and myself.

* *

In 1982, colour television (TV) was introduced in India. Doordarshan (DD) had a monopoly over the Indian airwaves and had started its national colour telecast in anticipation of the Asian Games held in November of that year. From that point on, DD became a desirable platform for advertising on a national scale.

In 1986, HTA was handling a serial called *Bahadur Shah Zafar* and mooted the idea of a sponsorship. The cast was stellar, with the lengendary Ashok Kumar in the title role, supported by Raj Babbar and Juhi Chawla and songs by Anuradha Paudwal and Mahendra Kapoor. The Munjal brothers mulled it over and pointed out that the serial was themed on the rather depressing subject of the last Mughal Emperor, who had been deposed and exiled and had his family decimated. They were reluctant to invest in the venture.

They changed their minds once they discovered that the serial was being produced by a Punjabi refugee father-son duo, very much like them: B.R. Chopra and his son Ravi. Mr Rai recalls, 'O.P. Munjal had a poetic inclination and an immense respect for B.R. Chopra as a fellow Punjabi who had fled Pakistan during the Partition. In fact, B.R. Chopra was not finding any sponsors for the serial and telephoned Brijmohanji.'

It was gently pointed out to my uncle that Bahadur Shah Zafar had been a poet par excellence and had produced ghazals that were timeless classics. This was my uncle's soft spot. He spoke to his '*bade bhrataji*' and the two decided to support Chopra. HTA's pointman, Kamal Oberoi, was summoned and handed a cheque of ₹65 lakh – a substantial sum in those days – drawn on the Bank of America. In keeping with the group's work ethic, once the decision was made, funds were released instantly.

Bahadur Shah Zafar was struggling to stay afloat until Hero decided to back it. From the moment it went on air, it was clear that it would become a spectacular hit. Ashok Kumar's performance received rave reviews and the series acquired a cult following. The Hero logo streamed into TV-owning households across the country.

The rapport with B.R. Chopra was to prove rewarding, when he launched his next venture: a 100-episode TV series called *Mahabharata*. No entertainment programme in the history of television has had a comparable impact. It began airing in 1988 and quickly became a national addiction, penetrating almost every home in India. On Sunday mornings roads across the country would be more than ordinarily deserted, as families clustered around the TV in their living rooms. In many places, station masters of the Indian Railways were coerced by passengers into prolonging train stoppages, so that they could troop into the waiting rooms to watch the serial! Mythology had been a theme of Bollywood cinema since its inception, but *Mahabharata* became a popular culture juggernaut.

Along with the tinsel crowns, blingy costumes and special effects, TV audiences subconsciously registered the Hero logo and during the commercial breaks, they were introduced to Hero's iconic television commercial. In terms of brand-building, it was sheer gold. Along with developing a superior product, in terms of technology and functionality, the *Mahabharata* spot made Hero the premier name in bicycles, outdistancing competitors by many a mile. It also helped in prising open a whole new market for what were popularly dubbed then as ‘fancy cycles’.

‘We had tried to break the hold of the tried-and-tested black-and-green Roadster bicycle. It was a high-demand product, not permitting any chance to manoeuvre customer price,’ Mr Rai recalled. Hero brought a European-style bicycle to India, with a version called the ‘Ranger’. ‘HTA played a significant role in product styling, market research and the launch ... this was a first for Hero,’ he added.

Demand went through the roof as the Indian bicycle industry had not witnessed something like this before. Dealers were lining up to place orders and were more than willing to make payments ahead of product delivery. ‘Dealers would come and place early orders, since they were paid by customers in advance. Some would even call Mr Munjal to fulfil their needs and get their deliveries expedited,’ Mr Rai recalled.

A whole new range of bicycles was launched, covering all consumer segments from kids to ladies to high end. Suddenly there were all kinds of variants in the bicycle sector. Our people on the shop floor and the creative geniuses at HTA worked in tandem to bring about the transformation of the bicycle industry in India. ‘Engineering satisfaction’ became the catchphrase of the company.

More to the point, Hero had introduced the ‘wow factor’ into cycling, romanticizing what until then had been a symbol of the working classes. The new range became a lifestyle statement, introducing consumers to the idea of the cycle as a recreational vehicle and an adjunct to good health. Unlike brands that had acquired dominance in a monopoly situation, Hero had done so in a competitive environment.

So well-loved a client did Hero Cycles become that HTA used it as a training ground. To head a department at HTA, you had to have done a stint at Hero and earned your creative spurs there. Tarun Rai, the group CEO of J. Walter Thompson at the time of writing (HTA became JWT-India in 2002, then went back to its pre-1970 name,

J. Walter Thompson), started his career as a part of the team that played a key role in Hero's image makeover. He later confided to his colleagues that Hero had taught him what passion and commitment could achieve.

Hero Cycles pedalled along with HTA, with the occasional bumps in their journey together. The group worked with other agencies as well, Lintas among them, but the HTA relationship and the one subsequently developed with Contract Advertising, which was an associate firm of HTA, were special. Late one night, my uncle called Mr Rai. He was perturbed at the crisis in Sunil Dutt's family, following his son Sanjay's arrest in 1993 for his alleged role in the 1993 Bombay (as Mumbai was then called) bomb blasts. Like most people who knew the family, uncle Om Prakash didn't for a minute believe that the thirty-four-year-old actor had been involved, and wanted to do his bit for him. Sanjay had been at Lawrence School, Sanawar, with his son and he had grown very fond of the lad during his school days. He believed he was more sinned against than sinning.

He told Mr Rai that he wanted to help Sanjay make his comeback and the only assistance he could offer was to make the actor Hero Cycle's brand ambassador. My uncle decided to sign him up for the role, for what was considered an obscene amount those days. He wanted a campaign for Hero's Champion cycle built around Sanjay Dutt and was keen on engaging Contract Advertising, which had carved a niche for itself in those days for its creative advertising.

Sanjay became the first of many Bollywood stars to advertise for the many Hero Group products. Rani Mukherjee, Hrithik Roshan and Ameesha Patel would all appear in advertisements for the brand, along with others. The pièce de résistance was Aishwarya Rai riding a Hero in Mani Ratnam's *Guru*.

* *

My father, meanwhile, was concerned with the sales of the Hero Honda motorcycles. The two-wheelers had been launched in 1984 with one of the most iconic advertising campaigns of all time. The 'Fill it, Shut it, Forget it' tagline – which was originally the idea of my brother Ramanji – exhorted Indian men to abandon their scooters and heavy motorcycles and ride the CD 100 which promised a mileage of 80 km to the litre. Actually, as per the mandatory pre-launch tests conducted by the Automobile Research Association of India (ARAI), the CD 100 was travelling 94 km to the litre. But my father insisted that the campaign should set a lower mileage promise of 80 km, in order to create customer delight and surpass expectations. At a time when India ran on scooters, it was an attractive pitch, revolving around the aspirations of the *aam admi* (common man) and the affordability of the product. In effect, it involved a massive shift of consumer preference.

By the mid-1980s, the Hero Honda was on the roads, but it was now time to rev up the throttle and boost sales figures. My father was keen to capture the urban and peri-urban market and then, the rural heartland. Hero would have to cast a net wide enough to reach every village and town in the country, which required a marketing plan on a summit scale for the auto industry.

The 'heroic' narrative was developed by positioning the motorcycle as a macho yet affordable conveyance capable of providing on reliability, rider comfort, reasonable pricing and low maintenance – which my father and Ramanji insisted upon.

By this time, HTA had developed a good equation with Hero, by imbibing the Munjal maxim that relationships built on trust and mutual respect were never purely transactional. Tarun Rai reminiscences: 'I believe Mr Munjal (O.P.) got the best out of us because of his relationship with us. He interacted with us both as the professionals we were and also at a personal level. Inviting us to make a big presentation when he was holidaying somewhere in the mountains of Kashmir or Himachal Pradesh – became an annual ritual.

'As Om Prakashji said, this was his way of mixing business with a little holiday for us. He even wanted us to get our spouses, having met my wife a few times. Once we met at Barog – a quiet hill station near

Chandigarh – where we had a nice lunch with him and Mrs Munjal. I was warmly hugged when I told him about the birth of our daughter. Of course, he sent me back with a gift for her.

'Talking of gifts – we came back from Ludhiana carrying gifts after every visit. Gifts for us and also for some of the creative people who had worked on the campaign we had presented. Small things that went a long way in building a lasting relationship.'

Incidentally, the practice of giving gifts is an old one in our business family; in fact, we've always given practical gifts, ones that are useful in people's home.

On the strength of the relationship that had developed with my uncle and his team, HTA secured the Hero Honda account. This company was a different ball game altogether, and differed sharply in its marketing approach. Unlike Hero Cycles, it had a full-fledged marketing department headed by Amit Chaturvedi. The Hero Honda account was handled by the HTA team of Colvyn Harris and Navroze Dhondi who developed a great equation with Amit and the team.

The marketing team came up with the idea of the Hero Cup. My father, who followed cricket with a passion, was struck by the idea. He would watch games, even in the office, during the lunch break. The staff on his floor would cluster around him and they would watch together and analyse each player's performance. In fact, over the years, my father developed a close bond with his front-office manager, Vijaya Chaudhry and his peon, Anand, who were completely devoted to him.

* *

Given Hero's association with the community, my father and uncles felt it would be a good idea to use sports as a vehicle to build the brand. Cricketing events in the past had been mainly sponsored by either insurance or tobacco companies. Hero became the first company in the consumer durables market to enter the arena of competitive sports. For all his love of cricket, Brijmohan Lall Munjal was not easily convinced and it took HTA many meetings and much hand-holding to entice him into biting the bullet. The cost of sponsorship, they pointed out persuasively, was a steal from the perspective of the traction it would offer. Bear in mind that in the early 1990s, there were only a handful of channels, a lot less money in cricket and very few takers for sponsorship.

My father allowed himself to be persuaded and, in 1993, the Hero Cup made its debut. It was broadcast on the Star TV network. As fate would have it – and to my father's everlasting joy – India won the cup. It will always be remembered in cricketing history for Jonty Rhodes' record-setting five catches for South Africa against the West Indies, Sachin Tendulkar's last over against South Africa in the semi-final, and Anil Kumble's match-winning six wickets for India in the final against the West Indies. At the end of an unforgettable match, Mohammad Azarhuddin held aloft the Hero Cup at Eden Gardens in Calcutta (renamed Kolkata in 2001).

Hero would go on to have an enduring presence in sports. The Hero Cup whetted the group's appetite for cricket and the Munjal brothers put their talent for spotting emerging talent to good use. Uncle Om Prakash happened to spot Irfan Pathan's bowling action on TV in January 2006 when he took a hat-trick against Pakistan. Uncle was so enamoured that he called up HTA and instructed them to sign Pathan up at once.

The agency had learnt the hard way that when O.P. wanted something done right away, he meant it. If they failed to deliver, all his fuzzy warmth would dissolve into an outburst of temper. So when HTA discovered that Irfan was with the Indian cricket team in Pakistan, where it was playing after a gap of fifteen years (the resumption in cricketing ties had taken place courtesy Atal Bihari Vajpayee's peace initiative earlier that year), they dispatched an employee to chase him down in Karachi. Only after the deal had been signed and sealed did they call 'O.P.'

'We had Irfan gainfully employed for the next five years at what today would seem like an incredibly low price,' recalls Mr Rai.

Our involvement in sports allowed us to oblige our network of friends and business associates – bankers, diplomats, bureaucrats, etc., by inviting them to exciting events. It was the only way we could express our regard for them, because we had stopped the practice of Diwali gifting early on.

Hero set a trend for cricket sponsorship by Indian companies, not just in India but also overseas. In fact, after Hero's massive entry into cricket, other sports followed. In subsequent years, Hero would become a enduring presence in sports thereafter, sponsoring not just cricket but hockey, football and golf. Golf, incidentally, was and still remains a special focus of Pawan, and the legendary Tiger Woods is associated with Brand Hero.

Despite being one of the largest supporters of sports, we never interfered in the game. We could have asked for a place on any of the supervisory boards and they would have been glad to have us, but we consciously chose not to influence the organizations managing cricket. When cricket governance began to look messy, we just pulled back our sponsorships. Our philosophy was to extend financial support, on the assumption that it would not be abused. In fact, as I mentioned earlier, we then started getting involved in sponsoring and supporting sports that were not getting any backing, such as hockey, soccer, women's football and others.

* *

A key component in brand-building was the great emphasis my father placed on customer-facing systems. The spacious showrooms, the well-informed and gracious dealers, the CRM (customer relationship management) schemes, were aimed at enhancing customer experience. The staff at dealerships were trained in the technical specifications of the products, so that they were never at a loss when customers asked questions, but even more importance was given to soft skills. Niceties like greeting customers warmly, serving water, soft drinks or tea and generally making them feel welcome could make all the difference to sales, my father told Hero's dealers.

Through customer engagement in a very traditional retail environment, my father managed to convey to them what he told *Outlook* magazine in 2006: 'Our goal was never profit alone but total devotion to customers; we wanted to give them full value and make them proud of choosing an Indian product.'

To this day, Hero is almost considered a generic for quality, reliability, integrity and affordability and ranks high on the brand trust index. It is a brand built not merely on a logo, a theme song and a slogan, but on the Munjal family values. To cite fashion designer Alice Temperley, 'You have to stay true to your heritage; that's what your brand is about.'

The focus on quality, people and customers inherited from Hero Cycles was deployed to create Hero Honda; at the same time, these were refined and merged with modern systems of technology and customer service. Feedback was regularly sought and care was taken to close the loops with engineering and design in each and every case.

My father made it clear, in no ambiguous terms, that all responses to complaints should be time bound, and ensured that the message filtered through the organization. Reputation and credibility mattered enormously to him and he personally tracked complaint letters from dealers and customers for many years. I remember him getting particularly peeved if anybody ever alleged that Hero's quality, or standards had deteriorated, compared to a previous period.

While my father got less involved in later years in day-to-day operations, he was, till nearly the end, personally involved in the final selection of a dealer. Over the course of a short conversation, he had an uncanny knack of determining a candidate's nature, value systems, and ability to keep commitments. More often than not, he was proved right.

My father believed that ethics, respect and relationships were the building blocks of any business and often said that relationships were like bank accounts: 'you will only get what you give'. This was the single most important premise upon which brand 'Hero' was constructed. As a 'people's brand', Hero implied a premium on relationships without compromising on numbers.

Ashok Kumar Taneja, chairman of Shriram Pistons, who described Brijmohan Lall Munjal as the, 'Father Figure of ancillarization', in India, said that he embodied the true spirit of *sabka saath-sabka vikas* (one with everybody for everybody's betterment) long before it became a political slogan. Taneja remembers him as the embodiment of old-world grace, rising graciously from his seat to greet a man half his age, even when he was in his nineties – this was a trait that was imbibed by all the brothers and later, by many in the family.

Just as my father embodied the uniquely indigenous concept of business *dharma*, Hero exemplifies the modern Indian homegrown brand with a characteristically human touch, an image sustained over the years and across new generations of customers and all stakeholders.

That old friend of the Munjal brothers, Kareem Deen the saddle-manufacturer, who gifted them a name, probably could not have imagined the grand success it would bring.

12

The Munjal School of Management

The Munjal brothers and the manner in which they managed their businesses became the subject of case studies, at many global institutes, including the London School of Business, INSEAD (France), Narsee Munjee Institute, etc. Their story has also been captured in reports prepared by the BBC and the World Bank Group.

Truth be told, however, the unique management concepts written about in these case studies were never treated as something unique by my father and his brothers. They had never consciously measured themselves against the surrounding milieu. It was the Japanese who showed us a mirror for the first time in the early 1980s. While some of what I write next may be a repetition from the earlier portions, this chapter attempts to pull the different strands together in the form of a management lesson.

On myriad occasions when I've been called to share the incredible Hero story with audiences around the world, I have always maintained that my father and uncles were merely practising common sense. It is a different matter, of course, that common sense itself is not very common. While it appears that modern management practices have emanated to India from around the world, at Hero, we've been deploying these practices for many decades, minus the jargon!

For example, from the very beginning, technological and process innovations were passed on to our suppliers and vice versa, and the gains that accrued from improved efficiency and lower costs would be shared. Only in Japan, they said, did companies have a similar depth of engagement with their suppliers.

Likewise, our quest for growth and profitability was inherent, and presumed. At our annual plan meetings, the question of whether or not a company would grow was never allowed to be discussed. It was assumed that the concerned company would grow and the only question was, by how much. All we knew was that we had to do better than the previous year.

My father could have written a management handbook for business leaders that covered corporate governance, human resources, inventory management, capital budgeting, working capital management and social responsibility. Had he chosen to impart his experiences, these elements would have surely found their way in his book.

KEY VALUES AND LEARNINGS

Perfection on the Shop Floor

My father and his brothers got the best out of people. An oft-told anecdote about my father and uncles is that they would sit on the shop floor for hours, keeping a minute watch on workers beavering away at a particular job. They would take mental notes of how many parts the quickest amongst them could produce in a given time. On the following day, my father or one of my uncles would ask the star performer to demonstrate his techniques for the benefit of his colleagues and encourage them to emulate him. They wouldn't stop there; once all the workers had upped their productivity, the workers would be told, on the basis of the elders' observations, how they could do even better!

My father and uncle Om Prakash spent hours with their managers and teams, discussing and encouraging them with ideas on how to narrow down production cycles and boost productivity. (Simultaneously, they took great pains to explain that efficiencies in processes were critical to making profits and generating resources to build the business, in which everyone was a stakeholder.) My uncle, in particular, was always looking for small improvements that would lead to greater savings and competencies.

As India inherited an economy of shortages post-Independence, cost consciousness was embedded deep in the psyche of Indian entrepreneurs in the decades that followed. My father would travel to Europe, spending days and hours observing machines and equipment and how they were designed and operated. He invariably picked up a machine or two and tooling processes were perfected back in Ludhiana so that the machines could be replicated in-house, at a fraction of their original cost.

While bicycles were sent out as part of a kit, every component had a separate assembly line that worked to clockwork precision. Accountability and responsibility were embedded; for example, the worker in charge of the pedal assembly line was also responsible for packing. Even in the 1960s, blackboards were placed alongside each assembly line, and every thirty minutes, a supervisor updated production figures, and mapped it against the day's target.

From an outsider's perspective, our productivity and attention to quality was outstanding. We had never measured it ourselves till then, but were informed by Honda when we tied up with them in the 1980s that our efficiency levels were amongst the highest in the world. The volume of business grew sharply in those early decades, but the number of people didn't. Over the decades, higher productivity and savings significantly enhanced our ability to attract and retain customers.

Over thirty years, Hero Cycles took the price of the bicycle from ₹200 to ₹600, even as the cost of inputs such as oil, paint and power went up between eight and several thousand times. When costs went up, adjustments were made in the entire value chain to manage them more effectively and in our pursuit of waste minimization and cost reduction, we would keep reinventing ourselves. For example, as demand picked up in the late 1960s, our managers and workers perfected a mechanism drilling five cranks together – replacing a cumbersome process that involved drilling in a single file.

We were also amongst the early ones in India to introduce mass customization – the ability to accommodate multiple product lines on the shop floor – without ever compromising on quality.

Our project execution times today are probably the fastest of any industry group in India. When we set up our two-wheeler manufacturing plant in Haridwar, from breaking ground to commercial production, it took us just seven months. Most people within the industry find it unbelievable and in 2007, when Hero was firming up a joint venture to make trucks in collaboration with Daimler Trucks of Germany, their teams had came over for due diligence and were taken to the Haridwar plant. They were amazed and told us that completing a factory of this scale in less than a year would not be possible even in Germany!

We developed best practices in-house or emulated those that we came across elsewhere. On his extensive travels abroad, my father kept his eyes and ears open, on the constant lookout for inspiration, and uncle Om Prakash was a stickler for detail, especially for improving throughput and reducing wastage.

Self-reliance

As a principle, the Munjal family was chary about adding debt to the balance sheet. Rather than knock on the doors of banks, the brothers preferred to rely on their own resources, which meant that capital for operating expenses and purchases was initially in very short supply. This cautious approach kept business cycles lean, improved profitability and mitigated risks. The Hero Group never found itself overexposed or facing liquidity issues.

As Hero's cash flows improved, the brothers also made it a practice to extend financial support to dealers and suppliers to meet their working capital requirements, on a case-by-case basis. In the early days, access to institutional finance was limited and, in any case, interests rates were almost extortionist. By giving channel partners a hand in difficulty or during times of crisis, we won a lot of goodwill and cemented loyalties. In fact, this practice of bridge financing our partners became a business for us and allowed us to develop a supply chain that was efficient and seamless and where spare parts flowed uninterruptedly to the factory.

The most significant outcome of tight finances and the focus on efficiency was the emergence of Hero's very own production schema, which the Munjal brothers later discovered was called 'just in time' or JIT.

Just in Time

The story of our much-studied JIT system begins with a lesson in history. Back in the mid-eighteenth century, India produced 25 per cent of the world's industrial output. Prior to the advent of the British, the subcontinent's share of world trade stood at 21 per cent, whereas that of Britain was a mere 1 per cent. By the time they left, India's share had declined to 1 per cent and Britain's was 21 per cent.

In essence, every bit of value addition was sucked out of the subcontinent to feed the industrial hubs and businesses in England.

Fast forward to 1956, when Hero Cycles was founded. The Munjal brothers soon encountered severe supply constraints. Bicycle parts were traditionally manufactured in Britain (and elsewhere in Europe) and imported into India where the English agency houses would then distribute the parts, allocating a quota to each manufacturer. If 1,000 cycle tyres from Dunlop, the global tyre giant, were imported, you could only make 500 bicycles and that was that. When the British departed, the agency houses were almost gifted to selected Indian associates, who continued their own form of the quota system.

Irked by artificial limitations on production, the brothers went around to their family and friends, suggesting that they set up component manufacturing businesses and become suppliers to Hero Cycles. The understanding was that Hero would not fund or run the business, but by working in synergy, everyone would benefit. There were three outcomes:

1. It created one of the world's most efficient supply chains.
2. It became the trigger for amongst the largest concentrations of bicycle part manufacturers in the world.
3. It allowed Hero to create its famous zero-inventory manufacturing system.

Our supply chain delivered exactly as much as was required on a particular day and not one component more, or less. We never offered an advance, but ensured that our vendors received their payments without delay.

We had no warehouses for incoming or outgoing goods, because we couldn't afford to have our capital locked up. The finished bicycles would be dispatched to dealers on a daily basis. Just as vendors took it for granted that their payments would be made on Saturday, the dealers were assured that the cycles would reach their outlets without delay. At the same time, they knew that they would not receive goods unless earlier payments had been cleared. Most of them would make advance payments, to ensure an uninterrupted supply.

Thanks to advances from dealers, we could pay suppliers on time without having to borrow and we always had deposits in the banks. What had started as a compulsion because money was tight became a strength.

In the initial days, since the business was low on funding, the supply chain was tightly managed and current assets were deliberately kept low. This system became so efficient that even when cash flows improved, the process of keeping inventories low continued. This practice of having negative working capital was unique. In fact, even today, it is comparatively rare to see working capital requirements being funded through internal sources, especially in the manufacturing sector.

We designed all our subsequent companies on the lean manufacturing principle, which was regarded as a characteristic of a few companies in Japan. So, when the Japanese came in, our systems resonated with their 'Muda-Muri-Mura', popularly known as the Toyota 3M model.

Right until the restructuring in 2010, none of the Hero Group's manufacturing companies, some of which were global scale, had warehousing facilities. In subsequent years, our flagship company, Hero MotoCorp decided to set up a fully automated global spare parts centre in Rajasthan, complete with cutting-edge robotic pick-and-place technology.

It was designed to capture value and revenue from volume of parts, and create a separate revenue stream for the company. It also ensured a larger supply of original equipment (OE) to counter spurious spares, which continues to be a chronic problem in today's aftermarket. At the same time, the global parts centre has ensured better service and enhanced customer experience across the dealer and workshop network, a message that my father kept hammering home repeatedly when he was actively involved.

PEOPLE AND RELATIONSHIPS

For my father, management was the art of working with and through people. When we hired someone new, we would try and assess whether their outlook on life matched the philosophy of the group. Those who couldn't fit in would generally quit in the first six months, but most would stay on for many decades.

His ability to manage relationships was legendary, but what stood out was the way in which he used the strength of his relationships during negotiations.

The value that my father and uncles placed on relationships is borne out through hundreds of incidents and anecdotes mentioned in the *Book of Letters*. Omkar Goswami, who was then chief economist of CII, wrote: 'You had visited Bangalore for the CII National Council meeting. You slipped out in the afternoon ... so later in the evening, when I was on the same flight as you, I asked you where you were in the afternoon. Your hair was dishevelled, your shirt was crumpled, and you had not eaten lunch. You replied, "One of our dealers had become a grandfather, so I had gone to bless the child; one dealer's son had got married, so I went to bless the couple; another dealer had lost his mother, so I visited him to offer condolences".'

Such was the value my father and uncles placed on relationships.

To resolve conflicts too, my father always fancied the relationship route. The well-known solicitor Jyoti Sagar recalled an incident when a top consulting firm recommended that Hero Honda should sue a certain entity, over an unsavoury incident. 'You (Brijmohan) said that till you were alive, there would be no messy conflicts and litigation. The issue must be resolved in a sensible and dignified manner', he said in a letter to my father.

We were and still are, all about people and relationships. This may well sound like a motherhood statement, but we genuinely believe that people are the only asset that appreciates with time. Even as far back as the 1960s, when the concept of industrial relations didn't quite exist in India, large trolleys with tea, biscuits and samosas would roll out across the factory floors for the workers, at 11 a.m., every day. The underlying emotion was one of warmth and camaraderie, and employees reciprocated in equal proportion.

In business dealings, my father taught us to always treat the person across the table as a friend. If you ended up working together, it would prove to be an advantage. If not, at least you would part as friends.

When mistakes were made, my father and uncles showed great magnanimity. For them, mistakes by managers, including family, were acceptable and even opportunities to learn, as long as the intentions were bonafide.

However, they were intolerant and unforgiving about malafide actions or instances of impropriety. The one thing my father and uncles didn't tolerate in people and we still don't even today, is a lack of integrity. We may be nice-guy employers, but any hint of duplicitous behaviour is unacceptable. I remember a Bombay branch manager being jailed for having skimmed ₹10,000. The fact that the amount involved was minimal didn't mitigate the offence; the man was our public face and his actions reflected on us, as a group.

Relationships were never purely transactional and, as such, given as much importance as profitability. Since my father mostly dealt with people whom he knew, or was comfortable with, he managed to extract quotes and costs that were way better than market rates; at the same time, he somehow managed to convince the counter party that the transaction was just the beginning of a relationship; so everyone went home happy! Once a partner earned his or her way into my father's inner circle of trust, he worked hard to ensure that the partnership remained for life.

As mentioned earlier, dealers and vendors who were in trouble would look to the mother ship for assistance. Uncle Om Prakash was particularly large-hearted in this respect. He once heard of a devastating fire, which had all but wiped out a major bicycle market in West Bengal. As a result, a number of channel partners lost their stocks and couldn't recover dues, which left them bankrupt. He stepped in and did all he could to rehabilitate them, even though they were multi-product vendors and not exclusive dealers of Hero Cycles.

My father and uncle Om Prakash always made it a point to be accessible to their dealers and vendors. It was never too late in the day to call them, whether it was to do with business or a personal problem. No visitor ever left uncle Om Prakash's office without a gift, which was usually a utility item. He used to buy them in bulk.

The ability of my father and uncles to create equal opportunity relationships and partnerships was a key bedrock of their legacy; under their watch, not a single dealer or a supply chain partner became insolvent. It is only when the generational change came at the top, did Hero Honda (now Hero MotoCorp) switch to the American model of channel and supply chain management with an emphasis on commercials and technology.

To be sure, there were times when such bonds were tested. For instance, when Hero and Honda parted ways in 2010, retaining dealers and vendors could have been challenging. Yet, there was virtually no attrition, thanks in large measure to the highly personalized bonds of trust and loyalty created over the years.

The Munjal brothers channelled considerable thought and effort into building fair and mutually beneficial partnerships, which paid off several years down the line. They were able to secure stock commitments from channel partners that would have proved impossible for others, thanks to the credibility they enjoyed.

'I still remember one discussion on the importance Brijmohanji gave to maintaining relationships,' observed Ajay Shriram, of the DCM

Group, one of the leading conglomerates of north India. 'His emphasis on creating a win-win situation was not only mature and fair. It was also very forward-looking.'

Thanks to my father's ability to make and nurture friendships and his insistence that we do the same, the Munjals had a vast network of contacts across the board, especially in government. We never used it though, other than to facilitate access when we wanted a meeting with someone. We would always put forward a proposal that would benefit the industry or the economy as a whole and pursue it aggressively, but never sought personal favours.

Leadership and Team Spirit

My father believed in inducting and nurturing talent. Over the years qualified, skilled and experienced staff were brought on board and great emphasis laid on developing teams and leadership skills.

My father often used the '*haath ki karchi*' (you are my ladle!) analogy while describing people whom he handpicked, but he meant it in a positive way; while the cook controls the ladle, it is the ladle that does all the cooking.

Many of those currently in key positions in Hero companies started their career with family firms and rose up the ladder. Mr Rai says, 'I was the first to join directly at a senior level. Strategic directions came from the top (mostly the Munjal brothers) in the early days, and there was no defining chain of command among the employees other than having a specific area of responsibility.'

Over time, the divisions became clearly demarcated, so that everyone knew where the buck stopped. This held true not only for promoters, but also for workers and executives and just about everyone. The top management always remained accessible, as long as they were approached with an agenda.

With every milestone came a lesson in management. It was from Honda that Hero learnt the Japanese emphasis and credo of team-building. If the environment was one-sided or tilted towards the owners or managers, there would be no team spirit. Hero henceforth made it a point to provide a comfortable working environment for all, in which the needs of all employees were kept in mind, from top to bottom.

Leadership was seen as a privilege and those vested with responsibilities could not escape accountability and both promoters and managers were expected to pull their weight. I still remember occasions when second generation Munjals were hauled over the coals by uncle Om Prakash for handing over the jobs assigned to them, to their managers. Thoroughly upset, he would roar at the offenders for burdening managers with extra work.

My father too, always protected his people. He would defend his managers to the hilt when Honda representatives or anyone else grumbled about them, making it clear that he believed in his team.

Simplicity, Transparency, Integrity

Long before KISS (Keep it Simple, Stupid) became a design principle, it had been internalized by the Hero Group. Managerial and operational processes were kept as simple as possible. The focus on absolute basics and drilling down to core values was in keeping with the family's inherent straightforwardness. Everyone, including family members, were encouraged to keep their speech and actions as open and as economical as possible.

Transparency in internal and external-facing processes encouraged fair play, enhanced credibility vis à vis all the stakeholders and maintained business and professional relationships on an even keel. The Hero Group inspired other businesses to adopt similar practices; many friends from the industry even consulted us to improve and gain additional insights for their enterprises.

After DCM was restructured in 1990, Ajay Shriram, referring to my father as a mentor, said: 'We three brothers (Vikram, Ajit and I) made sure we had a retreat every year to openly share our thoughts and feelings. At these meetings, I have often used Brijmohan uncle's approach and sought to emulate his actions.'

The principle of transparency was followed without exception. In the bicycle and motorcycle market, underhand incentives were practised by some in the industry, but the Munjal brothers refused to compromise and even admission on the subject was nipped in the bud. All rates were the same, and the essence of the relationship was grounded on the principle of equity. Managers, workers and channel partners understood and appreciated the philosophy behind this rationale because they knew it served their interests.

For us, integrity in business practices has always been non-negotiable and disproves the oft-expressed view that an 'honest businessman' in India is an oxymoron and I say this from experience. Nothing tested Hero's principles as much as Hero Fibres, our state-of-the-art spinning mill in Malerkotla.

I had been given charge of setting up the project, which was our first institutionally funded venture and one of our very first public issues. Even if I do say so myself, it was a mill like no other, but we suffered a big setback at the very outset: the strike of 1982, initiated by the labour leader Datta Samant led to the permanent closure of textile mills in Bombay and Ahmedabad. In one stroke, the bulk of our clients in the industry disappeared. All this happened just when Hero Fibres was getting off the ground.

The state government's promised power connection was delayed by a year and a half, but luckily we had got Japanese-made Yanmar generators installed. These, however, proved very expensive to run, particularly in a plant that operated 24 × 7, all-year round.

Our biggest handicap, however, was that we couldn't cut corners, not even a little bit. One of our competitors sourced his material from the same suppliers that we did and was ostensibly subject to the same import duties, but his cost was 30 per cent lower than ours. For us, fudging figures was not an option.

With the usual Munjal stoicism, we found buyers overseas. Every time a container went out, an inspector had to sign off and put his seal on it. We had permission for in-plant container-stuffing and the inspectors would pop across to our premises and do the needful. It was understood that they would be treated with great courtesy and given access to all our records, but that was it. No inducements were to be offered.

Our managers knew that this was the way things were done in all the Hero enterprises. One day, with a letter of credit (LC) running out and a recalcitrant inspector refusing to show up, they panicked and begged me to break protocol. I refused, without hesitation, knowing full well that the client wouldn't extend the LC and if the shipment didn't go out on that particular day, we would suffer huge losses.

As it happened, the fact that I was heading the Malerkotla Industries' Association came in handy. The authorities sent another inspector and the shipment was sent. Yet it could quite easily have been stymied and I was prepared to accept the consequences. My father and his brothers would not have had it any other way.

Focus and Open-mindedness

The scale of Hero's operations ensured that ideas floated in and out every day; some came from younger family members and employees, others from consultants and even more from a bevy of self-appointed advisors.

The patriarchs liked their concepts simple and resisted a constant shifting of goalposts. Radical thinking, of the kind likely to upset the applecart, was discouraged. Ideas could wait, they would always say and this was particularly true of those that were not in tune with immediate objectives. My uncle's laser-sharp focus on the 'here and now' kept the Hero ship afloat.

The fact that fresh approaches were subject to critical evaluation didn't mean the brothers were inflexible. They had no patience with fanciful, pie-in-the-sky notions but were always open to sound, practical ideas and once convinced, wasted no time in implementing them.

My father was remarkably open-minded, displaying none of the inflexibility and obduracy that often comes with age. He had the adaptability of a much younger individual and change rarely frazzled him; he welcomed each new development as a fresh start. From manual typewriters to fax machines to smartphones, he had seen and matched step with it all.

Consider for a moment his contribution to the literal and figurative mobility of women. For women in rural areas, the bicycle became an instrument of liberation as it was a means to get to school and acquire an education; to go to the market or get to their place of work without being dependent on a male relative. If nothing else, they could pick up a child from school or visit a relative. Mobility meant independence, the freedom to pursue whatever activities they pleased. Today, when women whizzing around on bicycles, mopeds, scooters and even motorcycles is de rigeur, I recall his insistence on a saree guard and polyurethane seats when our motorcycles were first launched to enhance the comfort of women riders.

The younger generation had the freedom to express their opinions, at the family discussions held over breakfast and dinner. I experimented with various ideas without telling my father and uncle Om Prakash, to get the proof of concept. I knew that if it worked, they would not reject it and once they took a decision, everyone was expected to fall in line, get on track and deliver.

For instance, they readily accepted the necessity of computerization, despite their old-school faith in physical books and discomfort with the trappings of information technology. Bear in mind that most of my co-workers, my father included, had little exposure to computers at that time. The fear that computers would replace human jobs was real and to their credit, despite their inexperience, they allowed the exercise to go on.

I began leading the computerization initiative and my father and uncles pretty much gave me a free hand. To introduce the concept and allay fears, we installed a few consoles in the Hero plant's cafeteria, with video games on them. Bit by bit, people got interested and then, hooked on the machines.

Gradually, as fears about computers began to evaporate, I mooted an Enterprise Resource Planning (ERP) system for Hero Cycles, which astounded my friends in the industry. An ERP was fine for an automotive enterprise, they said, but why would you invest in expensive software for a cycle company? Nonetheless, we designed one in-house, with the aid of a Silicon Valley guru, Charan Singh Lohara.

Our first ERP system bombed and I had to listen to a lot of 'I told you sos'. Still, we didn't give up and invited SAP, the leading enterprise software firm, to help up design another system. There was a fresh round of head-shaking. Not only were we investing in an ERP, but in the most sophisticated version available in the world at the time. The system worked like a charm but my benchmark for success was much tougher than SAP's; I would consider our mission accomplished only when Bhagatji started using the system!

That day arrived. Bhagatji was soon tapping away on the keyboard. But he often proved to be one step ahead of the computer. When we brought in NELCO and, later, HCL as technology partners, they told us they had never come across such a flawless inventory system in any manufacturing company, much less one that was maintained manually. Yet Bhagatji would shake his head over the figures churned out by the computer and say, 'This is wrong'. We would protest, '*Yeh* computer *se aya hai*', (this is generated by the computer!) as if that was the end of the matter. But he wouldn't budge and, each time, was proved correct.

Despite his initial suspicion of digital technology, uncle Om Prakash later became a convert. He was not an active user (he hardly ever used his mobile phone and never quite took to emails), and I remember hearing an anecdote about an earnest young manager, who came to him with a detailed power point presentation. Uncle Om Prakash told him to put his laptop away and explain the project to him face-to-face, without bringing the computer between them.

With time, however, uncle Om Prakash began to see merit in technology, so much so that he eventually began to demand inputs from the system for validation!

SENSITIVITY

For the longest time, the Munjal brothers knew almost all their employees by their first names. Since attrition was minimal, creating an atmosphere of conviviality was probably slightly easier. The brothers visited the factory floor several times a day and would make it a point to chat up anyone with a moment to spare (as long as it didn't interfere with their work). Familiarity bred bonhomie, and it also meant that their relationship with their workers evolved beyond business.

Having come through the mayhem of Partition, my father and uncles had a particular affinity for others who had faced similar experiences. Often, they picked their vendors, dealers and employees from among the Partition refugees. It was their way of expressing solidarity, by providing them with honest work and an assured income.

Success did not dilute their essential humanity or inherent humility. Everyone, regardless of whether they were at the base or the top of the hierarchy, had to be treated with respect and allowed to have their say. If you don't give them your regard, why should they return it they asked and believed that no one had a monopoly on good ideas. When the next generation joined the business, they followed the same code of conduct (the elders would not have permitted them to do so otherwise).

Hero didn't need an HR executive to conduct sensitivity training; all that employees had to do was see how my father conducted himself. He had no patience with trimmings and perks of chairmanship. At Hero Honda, and later Hero MotoCorp, rather than lean on the bell to summon his executive assistant or secretarial assistant, he would simply walk out of his office and brief him, or her on whatever he needed.

'It doesn't take anything,' he said when a visitor quizzed him about this practice. 'I would be sitting idle while he or she comes to my room. Why shouldn't I just walk up to them? In this way, I can even explain something if I have to.' His staff got the sense that they worked with him rather than under him.

On many occasions, the Munjal brothers demonstrated their value for their people by booking an entire cinema theatre during outings. The workers would be invited in two or three lots to see a movie, along with their families. There would also be sports competitions and rides for children during a carnival that would be held in December every year. In those days, it was quite a thrill.

My nephew Rahul (my late brother Raman's eldest son), remembers his grandfather as a perfectionist who had high expectations from those who worked with him. He set tough deadlines and followed up rigorously, but was not unreasonable if they could not be met for valid reasons. He also made it a point to leave his office on time, so that people working for him did not have to stay late.

My father never delivered a speech without crediting Hero's success to his workers and channel partners. He often described himself as a '*mukhiya*' or village elder and referred to them as his children. He always commended their work ethic and often declared: 'We are growing because you are growing; this success is your success as much as it is ours.'

On the factory floor, the Munjal brothers firmly believed that all workers were created equal. When McKinsey proposed a productivity-linked scheme, whereby employee performance would be linked with promotions, uncle Om Prakash opposed it vehemently. He said a person who was not up to par should quit the team; rather than be a part of it and get treated unequally.

At times, the brothers differed in terms of approach. While my father was generous with rewards, uncle Om Prakash was concerned about the impact of a selective system of rewards, because he thought it might destabilize the team.

The courtesy extended beyond the office. At home, any staffer who served him was assured of a smile and a 'thank you, *beta*'. When staying at hotels, he would make the bed himself and keep his room so spic and span, it was almost as if it hadn't been occupied at all. Housekeeping and room delivery staff would often be praised for their chores while he was in the room.

Environment

The Munjal brothers were sensitive to environmental concerns from the very beginning, a rare sensibility in those days and one that was founded on the age-old Indian belief that communities were an integral part of ecosystems. Long before the World Business Council for Sustainable Development laid out the obligations of companies to society, the Munjals believed that as consumers of resources, they had a moral obligation to maintain and conserve them. Accordingly, Hero's very first Effluent Treatment Plant (ETF) was set up four decades ago.

At the time, industrialists were not expected to have a social conscience and most manufacturers would simply discharge their effluents into public drains, without giving a thought to where it would eventually end up. The Munjal brothers realized that dumping waste water from electroplating processes would ultimately contaminate water bodies and perhaps even ground water. Expensive though it was, an ETP was installed and thereafter every time a new facility was designed, environmental concerns were embedded and ingrained in the planning.

Hero Honda was one of the early companies to use water-based paints, as is the norm in Japan and Germany. It was far more expensive in those days, but less damaging to the environment. We were also the first automotive company in the country to stop using asbestos lining in clutches and brakes because of its deleterious impact on human health.

Many years later, in a dramatic gesture which impressed our Japanese partners no end, the first Hero Honda motorcycle rolled out only after my father had quaffed a glass of water discharged from the ETP. And when Munjal Showa was designed, the power supply to the main plant came through the ETP. We knew that many companies had installed the mandatory ETPs but many did not run them; we wanted to send out the message that our plant wouldn't run until the ETP did!

Sustainability is now a catchphrase for industry, but when Hero Cycles was set up, it was neither mandatory nor did it offer a competitive advantage. The Munjal brothers were way ahead of the times in that sense. I internalized this lesson at an early age and when Hero Fibres was designed, I made sure that the campus was green in every sense of the word. Some 40,000 trees were planted and environmental safety norms instituted.

Work Is Worship

In spite of their advancing years, my father and uncles never lost their drive. Their constant refrain was: 'Many things still remain to be done.' At an age when most people were content to retire, they were constantly scouting for new vistas.

Even after the age of ninety, my father spent at least a few hours a day in office. If anyone ventured to tell him to take it easy, his response was unequivocal: 'When I am still on duty, what is the point of not coming to office? What will I do at home the whole day? I am being paid for this. What right do I have to not do a full day's work and still draw a full salary? The biggest thing is that I enjoy working. I enjoy coming to the office and I look forward to the day.'

Self–effacing

I remember former Infosys chairman R. Seshasayee speaking of my father at a public function: 'There are very few who have achieved success in business that you have achieved in a lifetime. Fewer have achieved success with an unblemished record. And I can think of none who has managed to keep their feet firmly on the ground while your head was tall enough to graze the stars.'

As a group, we have always been self-effacing. My father loved interacting with people, but hated blowing his own trumpet, and I hope that all of us have inherited that trait. We were reluctant to talk about ourselves, and except for our listed firms and consumer facing ones, little is known about our business operations and personal lives in the public domain.

Nor was conspicuous consumption encouraged. My father's self-deprecating attitude was visible in other ways as well. My nephew Rahul still remembers how his grandfather would buy cars of the same colour from a single company to avoid giving the impression that he was purchasing a new car! 'So we had one Black Mercedes replacing another or a dark blue replacing another dark blue!' he recalls.

In his values and outlook, my father was enlightened and ahead of his time, and often worked hard to ensure that others in the family also felt the way he did. In keeping with his early training at the ashram and his belief in the *Arya Samaj*, he stressed the importance of being detached when required. He believed that members of the family should be willing and able to act dispassionately when it came to strategic decisions like selling a company or exiting from a partnership, provided, of course, it made sense from a business, and family standpoint.

Sustaining the Legacy

It took me all of eight months to persuade my father that the university we were planning to set up in Gurgaon ought to carry his name. I pointed out that John Harvard and Nicholas Brown had lent their names to Ivy League schools. Stanford, Cornell and Yale were all named after someone. With the reluctant approval of my father, the BML Munjal University (BMU) was founded in 2014. My father had educated himself in the 'University of Life' and from here acquired most of his formidable managerial skills from interaction, observation, action and implementation. His education came mainly from observation and practice; these principles have been incorporated into the BMU curriculum to provide a practical and relevant education. The University is further based on the 3 principle Is, namely, Innovation, Sense of Inquiry and Impact on Society.

In our current academic system, a lot of time, effort and money is spent on an education that is of little practical use in our professional lives. Accordingly, the attempt at the university is to impart relevant knowledge, skills and values that give students a better chance at succeeding in the professions of their choice.

Above all, in keeping with my father's own methods, curiosity is encouraged; students are expected to ask the right questions, rather than learn the right answers. An experiential, cross-disciplinary and value-based approach allows students to take on leadership responsibilities at the University itself and, subsequently, at the workplace.

The learning on offer at the university is unique, with an emphasis on enquiry, creativity, problem-solving, entrepreneurship and innovation. Industry interface, innovation and incubation count amongst the university's key strengths, and there are dedicated centres on Automation, Robotics and Mechatronics, Advance Materials and Devices, High-performance Computing, Incubation and Inclusive Innovation. Siemens, Shell, IBM, KPMG, Microsoft, Hero MotoCorp and many others have set up facilities and centres of excellence on campus.

My father never went to college, but my earnest hope is that his life lessons will be carried forward across generations. If even a few of our students imbibes and incorporates his teachings, this purposeful venture in his name will stand fully vindicated.

Epilogue

Sunset of the Patriarch

A group of venerable gentlemen gathered on the quiet and leafy lanes of Greater Kailash every morning, to exchange views on life, the universe and everything. Brijmohan Lall Munjal had set that tradition. During his brisk early morning constitutionals, he would meet and greet other walkers. Conversations were struck up on the park bench and, over time, became a regular feature.

Age had not dimmed his bonhomie, though it did slow him down in many ways. He continued to attend office regularly even after he cruised past the ninetieth milestone. My brothers and I were concerned that he was taking on too much, but realized that keeping busy made him happy. The best course was to let him do whatever and however much he wanted.

On his own, he gradually cut down his workload, eventually by as much as 90 per cent. He would go to the office before noon and return in the late afternoon. Realizing that he had only so much energy, he didn't try and fight the march of time and accepted it with the same grace with which he had acquiesced to the partition of the Hero Group.

He insisted on conducting the final interviews for all dealerships. Existing dealers who visited the office would hang around, hoping for a few minutes with him. If he was in the office, they would be sure of being able to see him, because he never turned anyone away. If visitors came around lunchtime, he would invariably invite them to share his *dabba* (lunch box). The kitchen staff at home, aware of his penchant for sharing his lunch, would pack the meal accordingly.

Never a great trencherman, he had started eating so little that his doctors began to demand that he increase his consumption. Another worry was the threat of dehydration. His liquid intake had always been low, but had dwindled even further.

His tastes were simple. He had never smoked and was a teetotaller. All through his life, he stuck to the traditional daal-subzi-roti menu. He had a big sweet tooth, though. Every meal had to be followed by a bite-sized sweet, usually *gajak*, *rewari* or *khurmani*, which he kept in jars in the office and at home. His dinner was usually early and as Rahul recalls: 'His plate was as clean after the meal as before it.' It is a trait one finds in Sarvodayis (individuals involved with community development, providing upliftment for all, as advocated by Mahatma Gandhi).

He had always been a flamboyant personality. As a young man, he had dressed in style, ridden Harleys and tooled around in a variety of fast cars. He continued driving well into his 70s; he would consign his driver to the passenger seat and take over the wheel. He was a fast driver and thoroughly enjoyed zipping down the highways between Ludhiana, Chandigarh and Delhi.

Getting him to buy new clothes was a challenge. He kept his clothes so well, that a twenty-year old suit looked like it was new. He loved gifting, but never bought anything for himself. He'd lost a great deal of weight during his later years and his clothes were hanging on him, so I summoned the family tailor. I told him to present a few samples of fabric to my father, for a new set of suits. 'I have so many clothes in my wardrobe, I don't need anything,' my father expostulated. So I selected the fabric myself, because I knew his colour palette: whites and creams for his safaris in summer and dark greys, browns and blues for winter suits. After a bit of grumbling, he consented to wear the new suits!

He had always been gregarious and did a lot of socializing in the 1960s and 1970s. I remember him haring off to parties, with my mother in tow. As he aged, he began to spend more time at home. The family was so vast that it was a social circuit in itself and many of my distant uncles, or uncles by marriage, were his cronies. He also kept up with his old friends from his days in the CII and Rotary Club. People were his hobby.

After his morning walk and the *havan* conducted by my mother, he would spend a few minutes with the children before they left for work or school. At around 11 a.m., he set course for the office, where he would go through all his emails and letters, many of which were from people or organizations looking for funding. Nothing was ever brushed aside with a cursory look. At times, he would discuss the contents with his staff, or with Renu Bhabhi, who continued to share his office.

There were frequent interruptions as people walked in, taking advantage of the fact that he had always followed an open-door policy, literally speaking. (For the chairman of a large company, he had been remarkably accessible.) They would chat with him about anything from work to the news of the day to what was going on in their families.

In-between, he tracked the Hero MotoCorp share prices and if there happened to be a cricket match on, would watch it with the office staff. They took great pleasure in dissecting the match and players with him, to the accompaniment of jokes and laughter. There was always a buzz when he was around and his very presence would put smiles on peoples' faces.

He would head home in the late afternoon, to spend time with my mother. They would watch TV together and because many of those who figured on the news were his friends, he was quite accurate in his analysis of events. He had also begun to read extensively, mainly spiritual texts. He picked up my mother's habit of underlining meaningful passages, making notes and writing down his thoughts.

At some point, his memory began to fade. Names and faces became fuzzy, but no one who met him could have guessed it. He greeted everyone with affection and asked after their health and families. He could hold a full conversation without his audience realizing that he didn't remember their names.

In August of 2015, uncle Om Prakash passed away at the age of eighty-seven, at the DMC Hero Heart Centre in his beloved Ludhiana. Shortly after, my father began to wind down. It was when he stopped going to the office that we realized he must be really unwell. I received a call one morning, to the effect that he seemed quite ill. Like my mother, he wouldn't see a doctor without me, so I took him to the Max Hospital. He would never return home.

A full and satisfying life lay behind him. He had taken part in India's socio-economic transformation and, in fact, had helped to shape it. He had built the largest company in the business and touched the lives of millions. His children, grandchildren and great-grandchildren were well-settled. His life's mission had been accomplished. Ahead, lay another great adventure.

Deep down, I knew this but it was hard to let him go. He had always been larger than life, the moving spirit of the family and business. We got in touch with our friends in the healthcare field across the world, hoping against hope that he would rally and give us another year, another month or just one more day. I called Dr Inderbir Gill, a US-based urological surgeon and one of the best in the world, whose father had been the chief surgeon at the DMC Hospital in Ludhiana. He was deeply attached to my father and flew down immediately.

Our parents are not immortal, however much we want to hold on to them. I am reminded of the Biblical verse: '(He) breathed his last and died at a good old age, an old man and full of years; and he was gathered to his people.' On 1 November 2015, at ninety-two, Brijmohan Lall Munjal passed away. The family got together and decided that his final farewell should be a celebration of his life, rather than an occasion for mourning. We booked the Indira Gandhi stadium in Delhi for a memorial service, knowing full well that thousands of people would attend. Even so, the numbers were overwhelming. Traffic at India Gate came to a near standstill. India's top artistes, including Pandit Shiv Kumar Sharma and Hariprasad Chaurasia, rendered a melodious valediction, while Pawan and I read out four poems penned by Javed Akhtar.

Satyanand Munjal followed his brothers less than six months later. He was just a year short of *purnayu* (100 years). In the space of exactly eight months, all three Munjal brothers departed the physical realm. My mother Santosh joined her husband in April 2021 as I was putting the finishing touches to the reprint of this book. As we paid her tribute and homage in a sea of flowers, the outpouring of warmth and memories from friends and family members across generations during the virtual prayer ceremony simply overwhelmed us. She was my father's companion, confidant and rock as they went through life's highs and lows with incredible spirit. Partners in life and beyond, I am sure they are continuing their journey together.

Index

About the Author

Sunil Kant Munjal is an entrepreneur and investor with wide-ranging business, governance and policy advisory interests.

He is the youngest son of Brijmohan Lall Munjal, the Founder of the Hero Group. Besides setting up many new enterprises and providing strategic inputs for the Hero Group as chairman of Hero Corporate Service, he was also one of the managing directors of Hero Cycles, and subsequently the joint managing director of Hero MotoCorp (formerly Hero Honda).

As the Chairman of Hero Enterprise, he oversees diverse service and manufacturing businesses, and has made strategic investments in several areas ranging from e-commerce to hospitality both in India and overseas. Along with a few others, he has also helped create a base for risk capital, angel funding and venture funding in India through investments in digital learning, community transportation, healthcare, women empowerment and children's education. He has also invested in alternative asset management funds that take an entrepreneurship-based approach to socio-economic challenges.

He has co-founded BML Munjal University, a unique higher education venture that pioneers next practices in knowledge delivery and student development. He is also President of the Dayanand Medical College and Hospital, in Ludhiana, which has been ranked as a leading non-metro hospital and the number one private teaching hospital in North India.

He is Chairman of the Doon School, considered India's leading high school, where he also studied. He also sits on the boards of IIM Ahmedabad (IIMA), Indian School of Business (ISB), Shri Ram College of Commerce (SRCC) and University of Tokyo. He chairs the board of MEPSC, a government and industry supported skills' initiative to create a professionally competent workforce for India.

He sits on the boards of DCM Shriram, Escorts, Bharti Foundation, Indian Institute of Corporate Affairs and the advisory boards of Coca Cola India, Indian Angels Network Fund and UK India Business Council (UKIBC). He has also been on the boards of IIT Ropar, Life Insurance Corporation (LIC) and PNB Gilts Ltd and has chaired the board of Punjab Technical University.

He is a former president of the Confederation of Indian Industry (CII) and the All India Management Association (AIMA) and continues to be involved with them. He has been on the Prime Minister's Council on Trade & Industry and in the 1990s, he was a member of the Narasimham Committee that scripted India's banking and financial sector reforms. He was also on the Taskforce on Indirect Taxes (Kelkar Committee), that charted India's first roadmap for indirect taxes. He was also a member of the RBI's commission for labour reforms, and on the committee that defined roles for bank board members.

India Today chose him as one of the "Faces of the Millennium" for business. In 2016, he won the Jehangir Ghandy Medal for Social and Industrial Peace. In the same year, he was conferred a D. Lit by SRM University, Chennai, and became a Distinguished Fellow at the Institute of Directors. In 2018, Punjab University conferred on him the Udyog Rattan Award for role in the state's industrial development.

Sunil Kant Munjal continues his life-long love affair with the arts. He set up the Ludhiana Sanskritik Samagam, a cultural body to promote the performing arts in Ludhiana. He has co-authored a coffee table book, *All the World is a Stage* with S.K. Rai that chronicles experiences with India's finest music and theatre artistes who performed at Ludhiana. He has founded the Serendipity Arts Foundation which runs unique education programs, residencies and research in art and culture, and organizes an annual festival (Serendipity Art Festival) that has become one of the world's largest multi-disciplinary arts festivals in terms of scale, quality and curation of all art forms.